Legal Planning for Special Needs in Massachusetts

A Family Guide to SSI, Guardianship, and Estate Planning

Barbara D. Jackins, Attorney

authorHOUSE®

AuthorHouse™
1663 Liberty Drive
Bloomington, IN 47403
www.authorhouse.com
Phone: 1-800-839-8640

First published by AuthorHouse 3/17/2010

ISBN: 978-1-4490-8743-2 (e)
ISBN: 978-1-4490-8742-5 (sc)

Library of Congress Control Number: 2010902013

Printed in the United States of America
Bloomington, Indiana

This book is printed on acid-free paper.

About the Author

Barbara D. Jackins practices law in Belmont, Massachusetts. Her practice centers on areas of the law that affect people with disabilities and their families, including estate planning, Medicaid planning, government benefits, guardianship, and trust management.

Attorney Jackins has served on the Governor's Commission on Mental Retardation: Task Force on Public-Private Partnerships. She currently serves on the Board of Directors of the NWW Committee for Community Living, Inc., in Newton, Massachusetts, a non-profit agency that provides community housing to people with developmental disabilities.

Ms. Jackins is a member of the National Academy of Elder Law Attorneys and a 1978 graduate of Suffolk Law School. In addition to writing *Legal Planning for Special Needs*, she co-authored *The Special Needs Trust Administration Manual: A Guide for Trustees*.

Acknowledgments

Legal Planning for Special Needs would not have been possible without the help of many friends and colleagues. I am truly grateful to everyone who took the time to read the draft manuscript and offer their encouragement and improvements.

Attorneys Richard Blank, Mark Christopher, Annette Hines, Ann Jones, Linda Landry, Harriet Onello, and Ken Shulman generously offered their legal expertise. John Nadworny, a financial planner, reviewed the chapters dealing with life insurance and financial planning and made many helpful suggestions and improvements. Michael Herman, a CPA and tax attorney, made sure the tax information was correct. Harriet Barnett and Linda Davis Yanikoski served as critical readers for some portions of this book.

Stanley D. Klein, Director of the People with DisABILITIES Press, earned my gratitude for his support and encouragement for this project.

Last, I am indebted to my friends and the clients I have worked with over the years. Your unwavering devotion to your children with special needs was the inspiration for this project.

Table of Contents

About the Author v

Acknowledgments vi

Foreword *by Theresa M. Varnet, L.C.S.W., J.D* xv

Introduction xvii

Part I: Supplemental Security Income

Introduction to the SSI section..3

Chapter 1:   Overview of Supplemental Security Income 7

               What is SSI?
               Benefit Amounts
               Automatic Medicaid Entitlement

Chapter 2:   Qualifying for SSI 11

               Who is Eligible?
               Qualifying as Blind
               Qualifying as Disabled
               Resource Limits
               UTMA Accounts
               Income Limits
               Child Support
               Children under Age 18
               Children in Residential Schools

Chapter 3:   Reducing Assets to Qualify 23

               The Waiting Period
               Strategies to Reduce Assets

Chapter 4:   Applying for SSI...29

When to Start
The Application Process

Chapter 5:   Representative Payment...33

Should You Become the Representative Payee?
How to Be Appointed
Bank Accounts
Responsibilities
Where to Learn More

Chapter 6:   SSI Appeals 37

Why Appeal?
Getting Legal Help
Reconsideration
Administrative Review
Appeals Council
Federal Court
Re-applying for Benefits

Chapter 7:   Managing the SSI Benefit.......................................45

Avoid Repaying SSI
Appeals of Overpayments
Repaying SSI Benefits
Useful Strategies
What Can You Use SSI to Pay For?

Chapter 8:   Supplementing SSI 53

SSI and Independent Living
Sending an Allowance is not the Answer
Three Useful Strategies
Supplementing SSI

Chapter 9:   Work and SSI..61

Excluded Student Earnings
Earned Income Exclusion

Impairment-Related Work Expenses
Plan To Achieve Self-Support (PASS)

Chapter 10:   SSDI, Medicare, Medicaid, and Related Programs ..67

Social Security Disability Insurance (SSDI)
Medicare
Medicaid (MassHealth)
Adult Family Care Program
Personal Care Attendant Program

Part II: Guardianship

Introduction to the Guardianship Section....................................85

Chapter 11:   Guardianship Basics...87

What is Guardianship?
Deciding Whether Guardianship is Necessary

Chapter 12:   Alternatives to Guardianship......................................91

Release and Authorization for Medical Information
Health Care Proxy
Durable Power of Attorney

Chapter 13:   Legal Requirements to Obtain Guardianship..........97

Legal Standards
Limited and General Guardianship
Will Both Parents be the Guardians?
The Public Benefits Dilemma

Chapter 14:   The Court Process 103

Getting Legal Help
Court Forms
Filing the Paperwork
Legal Notice
The Hearing
The Decree

Chapter 15: Special Situations 111

Antipsychotic Medications
The *Rogers* Process
Extraordinary Medical Treatments
Emergency Guardianship

Chapter 16: The Guardian's Responsibilities 117

Reporting to the Court
Protection
Giving Informed Consent
Record Keeping
Guardianship Fees
Protecting Yourself

Chapter 17: Financial Management 125

Single Transactions Authorized by the Probate Court
Representative Payment for Government Benefits
Joint Bank Account
Durable Power of Attorney
Special Needs Trust

Chapter 18: Conservatorship 129

Conservatorship Basics
Reporting to the Court
Responsibilities to the Person under Conservatorship

Chapter 19: Frequently Asked Questions about Guardianship .. 133

Part III: Estate Planning

Introduction to the Estate Planning Section 139

Chapter 20: Why Plan? 141

What Could Happen if You Do Not Plan?
Plans That Do Not Work

Chapter 21:   Estate Planning Basics for Special Families............ 147

Do Not Leave Property Directly to Your Minor
Children or Your Child with a Disability
Who Will Receive Your Property
Depends on How You Own It
Estate Planning with Assets that Have Beneficiaries
A Coordinated Plan Works Best
Ten Steps to Sound Planning

Chapter 22:   Using a Will to Plan Your Estate 159

The Contents of a Will
What Information Does Not Belong in a Will?
Limitations of a Will

Chapter 23:   Using a Special Needs Trust to Plan Your Estate ... 165

How Does a Special Needs Trust Operate?
Personalizing a Special Needs Trust
Pooled Trusts: An Alternative to a Special Needs Trust

Chapter 24:   Communicating Personal Instructions for a Son's
or Daughter's Care 175

Directions Book
Side Letter to the Special Needs Trust
Letter of Intent

Chapter 25:   Planning for Your Own Incapacity....................... 181

Avoiding Guardianship and Conservatorship
Incapacity Documents
How Will You Get By Financially?
Special Needs Trusts and Nursing Home Expenses

Chapter 26:   Beyond the Basics... 191

An Unfunded Revocable Trust Can
Protect Minor Children
A Living Trust Can Reduce Probate Costs
A Bypass Trust Can Reduce Estate Taxes

An Irrevocable Life Insurance Trust
Can Reduce Estate Taxes
A Family Limited Partnership
Can Reduce Estate Taxes

Chapter 27:   Life Insurance 201

How Much Life Insurance Do You Need?
What are the Different Kinds of Life Insurance?
Life Insurance and the Child with Special Needs
Life Insurance Trusts

Chapter 28:   Money Matters...209

Working with a Financial Planner
Protecting Your Home
Money and the Child with a Disability
A State Sponsored Savings Plan May
Be Coming to Massachusetts

Part IV: Loose Ends

Chapter 29:   Registering for the Selective Service........................223

Chapter 30:   Massachusetts Identification Cards.........................225

Chapter 31:   Chapter 688 Transition Planning for Adult
               Services 227

Appendices

Appendix A: Massachusetts Legal Services Offices and
               Advocacy Organizations that Assist People with
               Disabilities 231

Appendix B: Aging Service Access Points (ASAP) Participating
               Agencies 241

Appendix C: Antipsychotic and Other Medications Used to
               Treat People with Mental Illness.............................253

Appendix D: Medical Release and Authorization Form..............257

Appendix E: Authorization for Guardian to Delegate to
             Caregiver..261

Appendix F: Pooled Trusts in Massachusetts 265

Resources 269

Glossary 275

Index..281

Foreword

I am delighted and honored to have been asked to write the foreword for this book. Barbara Jackins' efforts to better educate parents of children with special needs is timely and very useful. As a long time advocate for persons with disabilities and their families, it is exciting to play a small role in recommending this comprehensive book to families of all ages.

Like Barbara, I am the parent of a young adult challenged with developmental disabilities. Being Jennifer's mom has been an education in itself. Children, however, do not come with a "how to" manual. When one has a special needs child, the "how to" becomes very complicated! What a help it would have been to have had a book like this when Jennifer was growing up. There were few experts in the field at the time and no book like this to read for advice and guidance.

Jennifer is now 42, and in the past few years, The Arc and several of my colleagues have written educational handbooks for families. However, none of these books have the personal touches that Barbara has included. *Legal Planning for Special Needs* is easy to read, thorough, and comprehensive.

While writing a will is important, it is absolutely essential that any will include a special needs trust! Our children should not lose critically needed government assistance programs at a time when they need them the most. Barbara's book goes beyond the importance of special needs trusts, however.

Barbara reviews several important topics: how to save money for your child's future in a way that will not jeopardize government benefits, and why it is so important for your child to have a guardian, an agent under a durable power of attorney, or other personal representative to help your child negotiate the system after he or she reaches adulthood at age eighteen. She also does an excellent job in helping families better understand the SSI and SSDI programs. These two programs can be quite intimidating. Barbara explains the differences between these two benefit programs, including the eligibility requirements, the application process, and the appeals rules. Both SSI and SSDI can play a crucial role in our children's future, and every advocate needs to thoroughly understand these programs.

Legal Planning for Special Needs in Massachusetts is an excellent planning guide. Parents of children with special needs and the individuals we hope will look out for and advocate for our children when we are no longer able to care and advocate for them will benefit by having this book at hand.

I recommend that families pick up two copies—one to keep on their own shelf at home to refer to when needed, and one to give to the person or persons they have chosen to advocate or serve as guardian or trustee of a special needs trust for their child when the parent is no longer on the scene.

You will enjoy this book and find it a useful resource guide to refer to again and again. Barbara has truly made a great contribution to families of children with special needs by taking the time and effort to write this book.

Theresa M. Varnet, L.C.S.W., J.D.
Spain, Spain & Varnet, P.C., Chicago IL and
Fletcher, Tilton & Whipple, P.C., Worcester, MA

Introduction

THIS BOOK IS FOR PARENTS of children with special needs. It is intended to explain in practical terms how you can develop a sound plan for your son's or daughter's future.

It doesn't matter how old your son or daughter is. He or she could be a young child, getting ready to graduate from special education, or settling into a comfortable middle age. When you have a child with a disability, you can't leave things to chance. There is too much at stake.

I have had a disability-related law practice for over 25 years. During that time, I have seen firsthand how the failure to adequately plan can cause unnecessary cost, anxiety, and delay.

I first became interested in these issues many years ago when my son, who has developmental disabilities, was a young child. Like many parents in my situation, I quickly became immersed in the world of disabilities. As time went on—as happens with many parents—my circumstances influenced the work I chose to do. Eventually my law practice became almost completely centered in areas of the law that are important to families like ours: disability, public benefits, and estate planning.

Legal Planning for Special Needs in Massachusetts represents what I have leaned in my law practice. Why SSI, guardianship, and estate planning? Because those areas of the law concern almost every family that has a child with a disability, and all of them require advance planning.

Consider Supplemental Security Income (SSI). Many people with disabilities will qualify for this government benefit program at age 18. But if a person has more than $2,000 in assets, he or she cannot get benefits. With birthday checks, cash gifts, and your own diligent savings efforts, it doesn't take much to put your child over the $2,000 limit. Start planning early to find the proper way to save money so that your son or daughter will not lose any benefits at age 18.

Guardianship is another area that can benefit from advance planning. Guardianship may not be appropriate for every family. But if you decide to seek guardianship, you should have the legal authority in place on or shortly before your child's 18th birthday. That way, you will be able to act immediately if there is an emergency.

Estate planning is another important area. Almost every family can benefit from having an estate plan. Having a proper plan can help assure a son's or daughter's financial security when you are no longer here.

This book is divided into four parts.

- Part I (Chapters 1 through 10) covers SSI. Part I includes the program basics, how to apply, and how to manage the SSI benefits after the checks begin to arrive.
- Part II (Chapters 11 through 19) covers guardianship and conservatorship. This part addresses the decision to seek guardianship, how to get appointed, and the guardian's responsibilities. Part II also covers the new Massachusetts guardianship law that took effect on July 1, 2009.
- Part III (Chapters 20 through 28) covers estate planning. This part includes information about wills, the special needs trust, and other important estate planning documents. I also explain the correct way—and the wrong way—to save money for your son or daughter with a disability.
- Part IV (Chapters 26 through 29) ties up some loose ends: registration for the Selective Service, Massachusetts identifications cards, and the Chapter 688 transition process.

I also want to explain what *Legal Planning for Special Needs in Massachusetts* is not. This book is not intended to be a substitute for the services of qualified professionals. Instead, this book is a guide to working with professionals such as attorneys, financial advisors, accountants, and tax consultants. *Legal Planning* does not attempt to address every conceivable situation that could come up. All families are unique, and different circumstances require different approaches.

Another point: The laws and procedures in this area are quite complicated. Questions are bound to arise, and you will probably need qualified professionals to answer some of them. Be sure not to hire just anyone. Ensure that the person is knowledgeable about special needs and experienced in working with families like yours.

How can you find a qualified professional? Start by asking your family and friends. Perhaps someone has worked with a professional he or she can recommend. The Arcs (formerly called Associations for Retarded Citizens) and other organizations that assist families can be another good referral source. There are also some suggestions in the Resource section.

A last point: This book explains the current laws and procedures. Of course, those laws and procedures may change over time. I will update this book periodically to reflect those changes. Another way for you to stay on top of new developments is to attend some of the informative workshops sponsored by the Arcs and other organizations that assist people with disabilities. You can find an Arc in your area by contacting the Arc of Massachusetts (http://www.arcmass.org, telephone 781-891-6270).

I hope the information in this book is useful to you. If you have any questions about what you read here, don't hesitate to seek the advice of a qualified attorney. You can benefit from developing a relationship with someone who can assist you and your family. After all, there is no substitute for sound personal legal advice.

Part I: Supplemental Security Income

MANY 18 YEAR OLDS WITH DISABILITIES can qualify for Supplemental Security Income (SSI) benefits. This means that every month your son or daughter could receive a government check for several hundred dollars. However, the SSI programs rules are quite complicated, and you could get tripped up. It's easy to do.

The advice in this section is derived from my many years of experience representing people who have public benefits problems. The most common way people get into trouble with the Social Security Administration is by underestimating the tremendous power of that agency. Some people who receive public benefits have the attitude that the program requirements—such as the strict limits on assets—are not all that important. Even if you slip up, they assume, the agency will probably look the other way and take care of you.

This attitude can lead to trouble. In fact, the SSI rules are quite rigid and consistently enforced. A person's SSI benefits can be stopped for seemingly trivial reasons, such as not submitting routine paperwork in a timely manner. This can happen even though it is obvious that the person still has a disability and qualifies for benefits. Some recipients may have to repay thousands of dollars in benefits they previously received. This can occur even when there is fairly minor infraction, like letting the bank balance drift up to $2,500 for a few months instead of staying at or below the $2,000 limit.

I am not telling you this to discourage you from seeking benefits for your son or daughter. I believe that SSI is a worthwhile program. It's true that the SSI rules are complicated, and it's easy to make a mistake. But if you have a solid understanding of the program rules—and a healthy respect for the power of the Social Security Administration— you can avoid most pitfalls and keep the benefits arriving every month. My purpose, therefore, is to describe the SSI program rules in an accurate and understandable way to avoid any interruption in your son's or daughter's benefits.

What does this part cover?

Chapters 1 and 2 explain some of the basics, such as how to qualify, what is meant by having a "disability," and that all-important question, how much will your son or daughter receive?

The proper way to reduce one's assets to qualify for SSI is a subject that sometimes comes up in my practice. Often well-intentioned parents, acting on the advice of financial planners, diligently save money for their child with a disability through Uniform Transfers to Minors Act (UTMA) bank accounts or similar arrangements. Then those arrangements must be undone because of SSI's strict $2,000 resource limit. Chapter 3, "Reducing Assets to Qualify for SSI," explains the proper way to reduce excess assets.

After you have reduced the excess assets to the permitted level, you will be ready to apply. Chapter 4, "Applying for SSI," walks you through the application process. If your son or daughter is denied benefits, Chapter 6, "SSI Appeals" explains the Social Security appeal system.

What should you do with the SSI checks when they begin to arrive? Should you spend them, spend some and save some, or put them all aside for a rainy day? The answers to these questions are important. If you make a mistake, your son or daughter might have to repay the benefits you worked so diligently to obtain. The potential pitfalls of managing the SSI funds are explained in Chapter 7, "Managing the SSI benefit."

Even if your child now has a source of financial support, you may not lose your natural parental impulse to indulge them. You may still insist on paying for their summer vacation or buying a bag of groceries. But did you know that Social Security has strict rules against some SSI recipients getting financial help? It's true. Some recipients are not supposed to get help with food or shelter items. If they receive any help with either of these items—even from their parents—SSI may be reduced.

This strict no-food-or-shelter rule can be troublesome if your child moves away from home. How can he or she be expected to live on just a few hundred dollars a month? The chances are, you may have to help support your child. Chapter 8, "Supplementing SSI," explains some strategies to help your child financially without risking the loss of SSI benefits.

Work can be another troublesome area. You hope that your children can learn to do some work for which they will be paid. But as earnings go up, SSI goes down and may even stop altogether if earnings are too high. If income is not promptly reported, Social Security can demand that SSI benefits previously received must be repaid. This may be true even though those benefits were spent long ago. Chapter 9, "Work and SSI," discusses the ins and outs of this complicated area.

Fortunately, for many people, SSI is not forever. If you have paid into the Social Security retirement system, your children's SSI benefits may end when you retire (or die). Then your children can begin to get Supplemental Security Disability Insurance (SSDI) benefits based on your work record. From a benefits perspective, life is easier with SSDI. The monthly check is usually higher than with SSI; there is no asset limit; and there is no troublesome no-food-or-shelter rule. Chapter 10, "SSDI, Medicare, Medicaid, and Related Programs," explains SSDI and programs that provide medical benefits—Medicare and Medicaid.

I hope these materials are useful to you. If you have any questions about what you read here, please do not hesitate to contact a qualified attorney. You don't want to cost your son or daughter any benefits.

1

Overview of Supplemental Security Income

Topics include

SSI program basics
Payment amounts
Medicaid entitlement

What is SSI?

Supplemental Security Income (SSI) is a public benefit program run by the federal government.

Most people age 18 or older who qualify for SSI can get a check for several hundred dollars every month.

To get SSI, a person does not have to show any financial hardship or special economic need. Eighteen-year-olds from middle-income and even wealthy families can get SSI. However, they must have a disability according to the Social Security rules, have low income, and own few assets in their own name. Some children under age 18 can also get SSI. However, the eligibility rules for children are stricter that those for people over age 18. Chapter 2, "Qualifying for SSI," discusses the rules for children.

Benefit Amounts

In 2010, most individuals who live at home with their families receive $536.92 per month. A blind person can receive $823.74 per month. Individuals age 18 to 22 who receive special education services and live in residential schools receive $704.40 per month. A blind student who lives in a residential school would receive $823.74.

The amount of SSI a person can receive every month depends on his or her SSI category. Massachusetts has 18 different SSI categories. Each category pays a different monthly benefit amount. In 2010, the monthly benefits range from $72.80 to $1,128.

A person's SSI category depends on four factors:

- living arrangement (with his family, in his own home, in assisted living, etc.)
- marital status (single or married)
- type of disability (blind or non-blind)
- age (under 65, or 65 and over)

The basic SSI benefit is set by the federal government and is adjusted every year on January 1. Some states, including Massachusetts, voluntarily supplement the federal benefit. This means that Massachusetts residents get two benefits—a federal stipend and a state supplement—in one monthly check.

For example, an 18-year-old recipient's $536.92 monthly payment would consist of $449.33 from the federal government and $87.59 from the state. (A blind recipient's $823.74 benefit would consist of $449.33 from the federal government and $374.41 from the state.)

The annual SSI payment amounts for Massachusetts can be found on the Social Security Administration website (http://www.ssa.gov) and at http://www.MassLegalHelp.org.

Automatic Medicaid Entitlement

Massachusetts residents who get SSI also receive Medicaid free of charge. Medicaid is a federal- and state-funded medical insurance program that is run by the states. In Massachusetts, Medicaid is called MassHealth. MassHealth pays for most medical treatments, including hospital care, doctor visits, and prescription drugs.

For adults with disabilities, MassHealth can be an important benefit. It is the only insurance program that pays for state-funded residential services, day programs, and special transportation between home and work. Chapter 10, "SSDI, Medicare, Medicaid, and Related Programs" discusses MassHealth in more detail.

What if a person with a disability cannot qualify for SSI, or receives benefits for a period of time and then loses them? These individuals may be able to enroll for MassHealth independent of SSI. Chapter 10, "SSDI, Medicare, Medicaid, and Related Programs" explains how to find out about this.

2

Qualifying for SSI

Topics include

Blind individuals
Resource limits
Income limits
Child support
UTMA accounts
Children in residential schools

To receive SSI, a person must have a disability, have limited income, and own few assets in his or her own name. This chapter explains these rules in detail.

Who is Eligible?

To qualify for SSI, a person must:

- be blind, disabled, or age 65 or older
- have limited income (initially, no more than $1,000 per month in 2010)
- have few assets
- be a U.S. citizen or have the required immigration status

Qualifying as Blind

To be considered blind, a person's vision in both eyes must be 20/200 or less, or the field of vision must be 20 degrees or less, even with corrective lenses.

If your son or daughter is blind, you should tell Social Security when he or she applies for benefits. There are advantages to qualifying as a blind person. In Massachusetts, the monthly award is higher ($823.74 for a single blind person who lives with his or her family in 2010, as compared to $536.92 for a non-blind person). Special rules can allow blind people to work and keep most or all of their SSI payment.

If Social Security denies that your son or daughter is blind, you can appeal that finding. Chapter 6, "SSI Appeals," explains the appeal process.

Qualifying as Disabled

To be considered disabled, a person must have:

- A mental or physical impairment or a combination of impairments
- The impairments are expected to last at least 12 months or result in death

The impairment must be one that can be verified through medical evidence and tests—in other words, the impairment cannot be subjective. The impairment must directly affect a person's ability to support himself or herself through work.

Social Security has set certain earnings levels to determine whether a person is capable of self-support through work. In 2010, that level is $1,000 per month for a non-blind person and $1,640 for a blind person. Thus, if Social Security determines that an applicant can earn more than $1,000 per month ($1,640 if blind), the agency will find that that person is not disabled and will deny the application.

Resource Limits

Social Security limits the amount of assets or "resources" that a person can own and receive SSI. A person cannot own more than $2,000 in resources. A married couple can have $3,000. Fortunately, not every resource is included in the $2,000 limit. Only resources that Social Security defines as "countable" are included.

Countable resources

Some examples of resources that SSI counts are:

- Cash that is not the current month's income
- Income producing property, such as an annuity
- U.S. savings bonds (including accrued interest)
- Stocks, bonds, and mutual funds
- Life insurance with a cash value of more than $1,500
- Most UTMA and UGMA trust accounts if the recipient is age 21 or older (These accounts are discussed later in this chapter.)
- Retroactive awards of SSI, which are not counted for nine months after they are received. A person who receives past due SSI benefits in one lump sum has a nine-month grace period to reduce those resources to $2,000 or less.

Non-countable resources

Some examples of resources that SSI does *not* count are:

- Personal residence (house or condominium)
- Personal property, such as furniture, household goods, appliances, computer, TV, and so forth, regardless of the combined value
- Automobile of any value
- Medical equipment, such as a wheelchair
- Assets in a Plan to Achieve Self-Support (PASS); See Chapter 9, "Work and SSI"
- UTMA and UGMA trust accounts, when a recipient is under age 21
- Funds held in a 529 education savings plan
- Funds held in a properly drafted special needs trust

UTMA Accounts

Accounts established under the Uniform Transfers to Minors Act (UTMA) can sometimes cause problems for SSI recipients.

What is an UTMA account?

UTMA is a way that a person can give money or property to a minor child but still retain some control over the asset until the minor reaches adulthood.[1] Under an UTMA, a person opens a bank account or other investment account in the name of the minor. No separate trust document is needed; the person opening the account simply indicates on the application form that the account will be titled as an UTMA account. The minor's Social Security Number is used on the account. The custodian (usually the parent or grandparent) manages the account and makes all investment and spending decisions for the minor. In Massachusetts, when the minor reaches age 21, the account belongs to him absolutely, and the custodian must release the proceeds to him.

Countability for SSI

UTMA accounts are not counted as a resource when an 18-year-old applies for benefits. As long as the UTMA account is still owned by the custodian, it is not considered to be a resource. This means that a person under age 21 can have significant assets in UTMA accounts and still receive SSI. However, when the recipient reaches age 21, all UTMA funds immediately become countable for SSI purposes. *This is the case even if the custodian is still holding the accounts and has not yet released them to the recipient.* If the UTMA funds, combined with the recipient's other assets, total more than $2,000, the recipient cannot get SSI.

Reducing UTMA accounts

If your son or daughter owns any excess UTMA funds and is nearing age 21, you may have to act promptly to reduce those assets. Chapter

---

1   These accounts are also sometimes called Uniform Gifts to Minors Act (UGMA) accounts. Massachusetts abolished UGMA in 1987 and replaced it with UTMA. However, some states still have UGMA. Thus, the term UGMA is used by some multistate banks and other large financial institutions that conduct business in Massachusetts.

3, "Reducing Assets to Qualify for SSI," explains some strategies for reducing these assets.

Income Limits

To obtain SSI, an applicant must have low income. Social Security considers three kinds of income: *earned, unearned,* and *in-kind.* The three kinds of income are described below. Regardless of the particular kind of income, Social Security disregards the first $20 per month. This is called the General Exclusion.

Earned income

When a recipient has any earnings from employment or self-employment, SSI may be reduced, depending on the amount of earnings.

Social Security disregards income that a student earns, up to $1,640 per month or $6,600 per year (in 2010). A student is an individual who takes classes each week for at least eight hours in college; 12 hours in high school; and 15 hours in a vocational setting. The earnings can be through a school job or a regular job during the summer and on weekends. Chapter 9, "Work and SSI," discusses these earnings in more detail.

In addition to student earnings, Social Security also disregards the first $65 per month of earned income, plus one-half of remaining earned income.

> John, age 23, lives independently and earns $500 per month in supported employment. Although the maximum SSI benefit for John's category is $788 per month (in 2010), Social Security reduces that amount because of the earnings. The reduction is calculated as follows:
>
> $500   earned income
> -20   SSI General Exclusion ($20)

$480	remaining earned income
-65	SSI earned income disregard ($65)
$415	remaining earned income
-207	one-half of remaining earned income
$208	countable income
$788	maximum SSI benefit
-208	less countable income
$580	reduced SSI benefit

John has $1,080 per month available for his self-support (earnings of $500 plus SSI of $580).

Unearned income

If a recipient has any unearned income of more than $20 per month, SSI will be reduced. Unearned income means any income that is not derived from employment. It includes:

- Periodic payments such as Social Security benefits and annuity income
- Interest on bank accounts
- Dividends
- Child support
- One-time benefits such as prizes, gifts, inheritances, and direct cash payments from a trust

If a recipient has unearned income of more than $20 per month, SSI will be reduced on a dollar for dollar basis.

> Susan, who lives independently, has income from an annuity of $500 per month. Although the maximum benefit for Susan's category is $788 per month (in 2010), that amount is reduced because of her unearned income. The reduction is calculated as follows:

$500   unearned income
-20   SSI General Exclusion ($20)
$480   remaining unearned income

$788   SSI benefit
-480   less unearned income
$308   reduced SSI benefit

Susan has $808 per month available for her self-support (unearned income of $500 plus SSI of $308).

In-kind income

A third kind of income is called "in-kind income." In-kind income is defined by Social Security as food or shelter, or something an SSI recipient could use to get either of these items.

If a recipient receives any help—whether a bag of groceries or financial help with rent—for free or at a reduced cost, the SSI benefit may be reduced. Social Security has a complicated formula to figure the amount of the reduction: The reduction is either the item's cost or one-third of the federal portion of the SSI benefit plus twenty dollars, whichever is lower.[2]

Sarah lives in a condominium that her mother owns. The market rent is $900 per month, but Sarah only pays $300. Although Sarah receives $600 of "free" rent, Social Security only counts $244 ($674 x 1/3 + $20 = $244). Sarah has countable in-kind income of $244.

For every month that Sarah receives reduced rent, her monthly benefit will be reduced by $244.

Fortunately, regardless of the amount of in-kind income, the SSI

---

2   In 2010, the federal portion of the monthly SSI benefit is $674.

benefit is never reduced by more than one-third of the monthly benefit amount plus $20 ($244 in 2010). Thus, in the above example, even if the fair market rental of Sarah's condominium were $1,000 (so that Sarah receives $700 of "free" rent), the maximum deduction would not exceed $244. Also, note that the reduction only applies to the federal SSI benefit. The Massachusetts supplement is not reduced.

If an SSI recipient lives with his or her parents and does not contribute to the household costs—as is the case for most 18 year olds—Social Security will automatically reduce the monthly benefit by one-third. Social Security presumes that the food and shelter are worth at least one-third of the monthly benefit amount ($224 in 2010) and automatically reduces the monthly benefit by that amount.

> Chris, age 19, lives at home with his family and gets SSI of $536.92 (in 2010). The original benefit of $674 has been reduced for the value of the food and shelter that Social Security presumes Chris receives free of charge from his family. To calculate the reduced benefit, take $674 (the federal portion of the benefit Chris would receive if he lived alone) and reduce that amount by one-third ($224.66) to arrive at $449.34 ($674 - $224.66 = $449.34). Add the Massachusetts supplement of $87.58 to arrive at $536.92.

Child Support

Child support payments that you receive from your son's or daughter's non-custodial parent will reduce the SSI benefit. However, with some advance planning, you may be able to minimize or even eliminate the reduction.

Calculating the reduction

It helps to understand how Social Security treats child support payments for an SSI recipient age 18 or older. The amount of the reduction depends on the recipient's age and school status. If the recipient is:

- Under age 22 and regularly attending school, college, or training that is designed to prepare him or her for a paying job, one-third of the monthly payment is disregarded, and two-thirds is counted
- Under age 22 and not regularly attending school, college, or training that is designed to prepare him or her for a paying job, 100% of the payment is counted
- Age 22 or older, 100% of the payment is counted

Social Security also disregards the first $20 of the monthly child support payment. This is because an SSI recipient is entitled to receive $20 of income per month from any source without penalty.

> Deborah is raising Ali, age 18, who attends a special education program that is preparing her for a paying job upon graduation. Ali's father pays child support of $150 per week ($645 per month).[3] If Deborah did not receive child support, Ali could get SSI of $536 per month. Social Security counts $430 of child support ($645 x 2/3 = $430) but disregards $20 of that amount. The reduced monthly SSI benefit is $126 ($536 - $410 = $126).

Strategies to minimize or eliminate the reduction

Below I list some strategies that will minimize or eliminate the reduction in SSI. Parents who are going through a divorce or paternity action and have not worked out the child support arrangements could incorporate one or more of the strategies into their agreement.

What happens when you already have a traditional court order for child support where your former spouse or partner is making weekly or monthly payments? In that case, you will need his or her cooperation

---

3   The weekly amount is multiplied by 4.3 to arrive at the monthly amount.

to modify your existing arrangement. When Social Security calculates the SSI benefit, the agency assumes that the non-custodial parent is paying child support according to the court order. The agency will not disregard the court order and calculate SSI based on informal voluntary arrangements the recipient's parents have made. You should also get the court's approval to make any changes. If your former spouse or partner stops paying, you might not have any recourse in court to enforce the voluntary arrangements.

With these caveats in mind, here are some strategies to consider:

- Instead of paying child support, the non-custodial parent could make direct payments for some of the child's expenses. For example, the parent could pay for summer camp, recreation costs, clothing, special therapies, or adapted equipment. The parent could also make monthly payments for an auto loan, gas for your vehicle, or other transportation related expenses. Direct payment of these kinds of expenses would not be considered "child support" and would not reduce the monthly benefit. The payments could be capped at an amount that would equal the child support the parent would otherwise be paying.
- The payments could be characterized as spousal support (alimony). There are a couple of caveats here. One has to do with income taxes. In most cases, alimony payments are taxable to the person who receives them and tax deductible by the person who pays them. (This is in contrast to child support payments, which are neither taxable nor tax-deductible.) If you don't want the alimony to be taxed, you and your former spouse could agree that the person making the payments won't claim the deduction. You also need to decide when the payments would stop. Unlike child support, which stops when the child reaches age 23 (at the latest), alimony can be considered permanent support. If you don't want a permanent arrangement, you could agree that the payments would stop when the child reaches a specific age, such as 22, or no longer lives with the custodial parent.
- If there is more than one child, some or all of the payments could be shifted to the child without a disability.

Jane has two children, Joey, who is 13 and has a disability, and Ted, age 17, who has no disabilities and will be attending college in the fall. Instead of paying child support for Joey, his father could contribute more to Ted's education costs.

Frank is raising two children, Jenna, who is age 18 and has a disability, and Emily, age 8, who has no disabilities. Under the child support guidelines, the children's mother must pay $1,000 per month in child support for both children. Frank could ask the judge to allocate $166 for Jenna and $834 for Emily. The rationale is that, under the child support guidelines, when there are two children, the amount of child support is about 20% more than when there are is one child.

- The payments could be made to a special needs trust. The custodial parent could be the trustee. (The trustee is the person who manages the trust.) The funds in the trust could be used for things like clothes, recreation, education, medical care, room and board, special therapies, travel, and hobbies. A caveat is that the special needs trust must be rather restrictive. It must provide that on your son's or daughter's death, any remaining funds will be applied to his or her Medicaid bill with the state. This means that you can't use the special needs trust your attorney prepared as part of your estate plan. Estate planning trusts usually specify that any remaining assets can pass to other family members, not the state. (Chapter 3, "Reducing Assets to Qualify for SSI," discusses trusts that can be used for child support payments. Chapter 23, "Using a Special Needs Trust to Plan Your Estate," covers estate planning trusts.) Consider whether it is cost effective to pay an attorney to prepare a special needs trust that will only be used for child support payments.

Children under Age 18

Your son or daughter does not necessarily have to wait until age 18 to get SSI. Some children under age 18 can also get benefits.

The disability rules for children are different from those for adults. The work test that Social Security uses for adults does not make sense for children. Instead, Social Security compares the overall functioning of SSI applicant children to that of same age children without disabilities. Essentially, Social Security is looking for a mental or physical impairment (or combination of impairments). These impairments must affect the child's ability to reach age appropriate developmental milestones or to engage in age appropriate activities of daily living, such as walking, talking, or playing.

There are also different financial rules for children. A portion of the income and assets of the parents who live with the child may be attributed ("deemed") to the child for eligibility purposes. For example, if a single parent of a blind child has savings of $10,000, her child cannot get SSI, because the asset limit for a one-parent household is only $4,000 ($5,000 for a two-parent household). These strict financial rules can make it hard for children to get SSI.

Children in Residential Schools

Some children (under age 18) who live in residential schools are not subject to the strict income and asset deeming rules that pertain to children who live at home. These deeming rules are waived if Social Security judges a child to be "independent" of his or her parents. Under the SSI rules, an independent child is one who lives at school during the week and remains at school most weekends and during school vacations.

If Social Security judges a child to be independent from his or her parents, the parents' income and assets are not counted for eligibility purposes. A child who meets the disability and financial criteria (such having $2,000 or less in personal resources) can get SSI.

In most cases, a child who lives in a residential school is assigned to the "shared living" benefit category. That means that he or she can get $704.40 per month (in 2010).

3

Reducing Assets to Qualify

> Topics include
>
> **Waiting period to get benefits**
> **Permissible ways to reduce resources**
> **UTMA bank accounts**
> **Special needs trusts**

To obtain SSI, a person cannot own more than $2,000 in countable resources. If he or she has more than that amount, the resources must be reduced. The challenge is to reduce the resources without violating the strict SSI rules that govern this area. This chapter explains how a person can reduce his or her excess assets to qualify for SSI.

The Waiting Period

The SSI rules prohibit an applicant from giving away resources to reach the $2,000 limit. If an applicant transfers a resource or spends any money, he or she must get something of equivalent value. If an applicant transfers a resource for less than its equivalent value, there will be a waiting period to get SSI.

The look-back period

When a person applies for SSI, Social Security looks back over the past 36 months to see whether the applicant has transferred any assets for less than their equivalent value. Any transfers that were made more than 36 months before the application date are disregarded.

David, age 14, cashes $5,000 in savings bonds and gives the proceeds to his parents. When David applies for SSI at age 18, he can qualify immediately for benefits (assuming that he has $2,000 or less in resources and meets the other program requirements). Social Security disregards the transfers David made four years earlier at age 14.

Calculating the waiting period

If an applicant transfers any assets without obtaining equivalent value within 36 months of applying for SSI, there will be a waiting period to get benefits. The waiting period begins on the date the resource is transferred. To calculate the waiting period, Social Security divides the value of the transferred resource by the monthly SSI benefit amount the person would receive if he or she qualified for benefits.

John, age 18, owns $5,000 in U.S. savings bonds. Just before he applies for SSI, he cashes the bonds and gives $3,000 to his parents. (John may retain $2,000 in resources, so the amount of the gift is $3,000.) John cannot get SSI for 5 months. (If eligible, John would have received SSI of $536 per month. $3,000 divided by $536 is 5.59, rounded down to 5 months.)

Fortunately, the waiting period is limited to 36 months. Under the current program rules, an applicant may not lose benefits for more than 36 months, regardless of the amount transferred. Thus, in the previous example, if John transferred $20,000 to his parents, he would lose SSI for only 36 months.

Also note that the 36-month limit for uncompensated transfers only applies to the SSI program. Other public benefit programs, such as nursing home-level Medicaid, have different rules for transfers of assets. In Massachusetts, a person who transfers his or her assets in order to qualify for nursing home benefits cannot get those benefits until 60 months until after the date of transfer.

Strategies to Reduce Assets

How can a person reduce his or her excess assets and not incur a waiting period to get SSI? Here are some strategies that might work.

Spend the resources

One strategy is to spend the money. This strategy will work if the amount in question is relatively small. You could spend the money on items your child could use and enjoy, such as summer camp, recreational programs, lessons, and special therapies.

But there are a couple of caveats here. One is that the money must be spent only on your child. You can't use your child's money to pay for a Disney vacation for the whole family.

If your son or daughter is under age 18, the money should *not* be used to pay for basic support items, such as food, shelter, and medical care. According to Social Security, parents are legally responsible to provide these items for their children. A child's own resources should not be used to replace the parent's legal "duty of support."

Purchase non-countable resources

Another strategy is to use the assets to purchase items that Social Security does not count toward the $2,000 resource limit. These "non-countable" items could include a computer, software, furniture, TV, clothing, sports equipment, and recreational items. A person can own these kinds of personal items, regardless of their aggregate value.

Create a special needs trust

If your son or daughter has more money than he or she can comfortably spend, the excess resources can be placed in a special needs trust. The SSI rules allow an applicant to transfer his or her resources to a special needs trust and qualify right away for SSI.

A special needs trust is a way that a person with a disability can benefit from a trust and still receive SSI and other government benefits. Funds held in this type of trust are not included in the $2,000 resource limit.

To qualify, a special needs trust that contains a person's own assets must meet certain requirements:[4]

- The trust must be irrevocable. This means that after the trust is written, it cannot be changed; although, in some cases, limited amendments can be made for tax or administrative reasons. A person who places his funds in an irrevocable special needs trust cannot change his mind and take the money out.
- Only the trustee—not the beneficiary—can decide how the trust funds will be used. The beneficiary cannot get money from the trust without the trustee's permission.
- The trust document must be signed by the beneficiary's parent, grandparent, legal guardian, or a court. Due to a wrinkle in the law, a person with a disability cannot sign the document that creates his or her own trust. This is not usually a problem for most 18-year-olds, because they are likely to have a parent or grandparent who is still living.
- The trust must provide that on the beneficiary's death, any remaining trust funds will be used to re-pay the state Medicaid agency for the medical services the beneficiary received while he or she was alive.
- The trust document must say that the state Medicaid agency will be the first payee when the beneficiary dies. Not even the beneficiary's funeral expenses have priority.

It is important to note that all the remaining trust assets do not necessarily revert to the state. The state is only entitled to be reimbursed for the amount of the beneficiary's Medicaid bill. If the beneficiary was healthy or had other medical insurance, the bill may be small. But if the beneficiary was hospitalized or lived in a nursing home or

---

4   The rules listed here are for trusts created on or after January 1, 2000 with the beneficiary's own funds. There are different rules for trusts created before January 1, 2000. There are also different rules for trusts that contain assets that belonged to another person—such as the beneficiary's parent—before they were put in the trust. Neither of these kinds of trusts require the government to be paid back when the beneficiary dies. Trusts that do not require the government to be repaid are covered in the Estate Planning section of this book.

similar medical facility, the state's bill could amount to more than the remaining trust assets.

You can minimize the potential payback amount by spending the trust funds while the beneficiary is living. The trust assets—instead of the parent's own resources—can be used to purchase housing, recreation, or other items for the beneficiary. When the beneficiary dies, little if any money will be left in the trust.

Reducing UTMA accounts

As I explained in the previous chapter, a Uniform Transfers to Minors Act (UTMA) account does not become countable until the recipient is age 21. There is a three-year grace period between ages 18 and 21 when the recipient can reduce the account so it does not interfere with SSI eligibility.

The first two strategies to reduce assets that were discussed earlier (spending the funds and purchasing non-countable resources) will also work for UTMA accounts. The law that governs UTMA accounts permits the custodian to withdraw funds under his or her control and spend them on the beneficiary.

But should a custodian place UTMA funds in a special needs trust? This is a complicated area where not all legal experts agree on what is appropriate.

The complicating factor has to do with the custodian's legal responsibility under UTMA. Under that statute, the custodian must release the funds directly to the beneficiary when he or she reaches age 21. But with a special needs trust, the beneficiary's access to his money is restricted beyond age 21, possibly for his entire life. That raises the question whether the custodian who places UTMA funds in a special needs trust has violated his legal duty to the beneficiary.

One solution is for the custodian to ask the probate court for permission to create a special needs trust and transfer the assets to the trust. A court order authorizing the transfer will relieve the custodian of any potential liability for his actions.

Another solution might be for the custodian to release the funds directly to the beneficiary. The beneficiary can transfer them to a special needs trust. This might work if the beneficiary is able to understand the significance of what he or she is being asked to do.

Regardless of who makes the transfer—the custodian or the beneficiary—there is a drawback. The special needs trust must contain the payback requirement discussed earlier that will allow the state to be reimbursed for the beneficiary's Medicaid bill on death.

If your son or daughter must reduce UTMA funds to receive SSI, be sure to consult a qualified attorney before proceeding. You don't want to make a mistake and lose any benefits.

4

Applying for SSI

Topics include

When and where to apply
Information needed to apply
The initial interview
Independent medical examinations

The Social Security Administration makes it relatively easy to apply for SSI. Here are some suggestions that may help the application be approved right away.

When to Start

To make sure that your son or daughter doesn't miss out on any SSI payments, plan to apply for SSI about one month before his or her 18th birthday. This will allow Social Security sufficient time to evaluate the claim and begin paying benefits right away.

It is important to apply promptly because Social Security will not pay any benefits until a claim is filed. A person cannot get retroactive benefits beginning on the date he could have filed (or should have filed), even if all the program requirements are met.

Social Security will not pay any benefits, however, for an applicant's 18th birthday month or for the following month.

> John's birthday is April 27. His mother applies
> for benefits on his behalf on April 1. John's SSI
> benefits will begin June 1.

The Application Process

You can apply for SSI by telephone or at any local district office. For information, call Social Security's main telephone number (800-772-1213), or go to the website (http://www.ssa.gov), which has a local office search. If you apply in person, your son or daughter does not need to attend the initial interview.

Information you will need to apply

Whether your initial interview is in person or by telephone, you should collect the information listed below and have it available for the interview. Be sure to keep copies of all the documents you provide, and also note the name of the Social Security representative you speak with.

- Social Security Number
- If your son or daughter is not a U.S. citizen, proof of his or her immigration status
- Your son's or daughter's birth certificate
- Copies of bank statements, U.S. savings bonds, or other assets that your son or daughter owns
- Information about your son's or daughter's current wages, if any
- The amount of rent or mortgage and real estate taxes you pay for your home
- The current cash surrender value of any life insurance policy that your son or daughter owns
- Any medical documents that support the disability claim, such as psychological reports, neurological exams, medical documents, or IQ exams (if showing IQ of about 70 or less, which is presumptive for an intellectual disability in Massachusetts)
- The name, address, and telephone number for the contact person where your son or daughter attends school
- Names and addresses of doctors, hospitals, and others who have recently treated your son or daughter and have information that will help establish his or her disability

- Name, address, and account number of the bank or other financial institution where you want the SSI checks to be directly deposited

What to expect at the initial interview

The initial interview takes place with an intake worker. The worker will ask you questions about your son's or daughter's financial eligibility, including the amount of any income and assets in his or her name. The worker will also ask you if your son or daughter has a trust fund. You only need to provide information about trusts that currently contain assets. You do not need to report a trust that you have established as part of your estate plan if the trust does not contain any assets yet.

You will probably be asked to complete a Disability Report. This form contains information about your son's or daughter's disabling condition, such as the nature or the disability, medications, and recent treatment at hospitals and clinics.

The worker will also give you several blank Medical Record Releases for your son or daughter to sign. These releases will be directed to your child's primary care physician and to any other doctors, hospitals, or clinics that have recently treated your child. Social Security uses these releases to obtain relevant medical information directly from third parties.

The worker will also ask you whether you want to become your son's or daughter's representative payee. As the "rep payee," you can receive the SSI check directly in your name to use on your son's or daughter's behalf. In most cases, you will want to become your son's or daughter's rep payee. If the intake worker does not mention becoming a rep payee, be sure to ask him or her about that option.

Social Security strongly prefers that all SSI checks be directly deposited into the recipient's bank account. You will be asked to provide the name, address, and account number of the bank or other financial institution where you want to have the checks deposited.

If the initial interview takes place in person at the local office, you will be asked to sign a computer-generated application and other forms and releases. Be sure to read the documents carefully before you sign them, and also obtain a copy for your records.

In you apply by telephone, the completed application and supporting documents will be mailed to you for your signature. After you sign them, be sure to make a copy for your file before you return them to Social Security.

To speed up the approval process, you can bring copies of your son's or daughter's medical reports and records to the initial interview. (Even if you do that, however, the intake worker will probably still ask for signed releases authorizing any medical providers to send those same records directly to Social Security.)

It may also help to write a letter in support of your son's or daughter's claim. The letter should refer to the enclosed medical records and highlight those portions of the records that substantiate the disability. In my experience, if the medical evidence of the disability is reasonably clear, Social Security may approve the claim right away, without a lengthy investigation.

Independent Medical Examinations

Sometimes Social Security may require an applicant to undergo an Independent Medical Examination (IME). This may occur when Social Security feels that the medical evidence is not sufficient to either approve or deny a claim.

An IME is conducted by a private practitioner (generally a physician or psychologist) and takes place at the practitioner's office. The local Social Security office will schedule the appointment and notify the applicant of the time and date of the exam. There is no cost to the applicant. The examiner's fee is paid by Social Security. It is important to keep the scheduled appointment. If your son or daughter fails to appear, the claim will be decided without the medical evidence and will probably be denied.

When to expect a decision

Social Security usually makes a decision approving or denying benefits within three months from the date of application. If the benefits are approved, Social Security will issue a check that includes a retroactive payment for each month of eligibility. If the benefits are denied, you can appeal the denial. Chapter 6, "SSI Appeals," explains this process.

5

Representative Payment

Topics include

Should you become the representative payee?
Getting appointed
The representative payee bank account
The representative payee's responsibilities

If an SSI recipient cannot manage the benefit payments on his own, a representative payee ("rep payee") can be appointed. The rep payee receives the recipient's check and manages it for the recipient. This can assure the SSI checks are properly accounted for and not lost, stolen, or mismanaged.

Should You Become the Representative Payee?

In most cases, yes. There are two principal benefits to becoming rep payee—control and communication. But there can be a downside too. If the recipient has been overpaid and is unable to reimburse Social Security, then in some cases the agency might look to the rep payee for compensation. Chapter 7, "Managing the SSI Benefit," explains the rep payee's responsibility for the recipient's Social Security debt.

Control

As rep payee, you can immediately step in and take charge of the SSI checks. This means that you can arrange for SSI payments to be deposited directly into a special bank account that you establish. You can write checks to pay your son's or daughter's bills and purchase any items he or she needs.

If you are not the representative payee, you might have to manage your son's or daughter's SSI payments as the court appointed conservator. This can be terribly time-consuming and expensive. Chapter 18, "Conservatorship," explains a conservator's responsibilities.

Communication

A benefit to becoming the rep payee is that the Social Security caseworkers will communicate directly with you about your son's or daughter's benefits. This is important because there may be times when you need to speak with Social Security on your son's or daughter's behalf. You might need to report information or follow up on a letter he or she has received.

When there is a rep payee, the caseworkers will deal directly with that person. Otherwise, due to privacy rules, unless the recipient has appointed a representative, the caseworkers will only speak with the recipient. This policy can lead to a frustrating scenario—familiar to many parents—where a caseworker, citing the aforementioned privacy rules, will tell you to "get your child and bring him to the phone."

How to Be Appointed

Perhaps a court has already appointed you as your son's or daughter's legal guardian. If so, Social Security will make you the rep payee automatically, without any further inquiry.

If you are not the legal guardian, Social Security requires medical documentation to the effect that your son or daughter needs help to manage his or her money. The information the agency requires is included on the questionnaire that is sent to the applicant's personal physician (often the pediatrician).

You should speak with your son's or daughter's doctor about the medical forms that Social Security asks the doctor to complete. Tell the doctor that you have applied to become rep payee, and explain why you feel that it is best that you—not your child—should be in charge of the money. In most cases, the physician's confirmation that the recipient needs help to manage the SSI benefits will be sufficient for Social Security to appoint you.

Bank Accounts

Under the SSI rules, a representative payee is supposed to open a special bank account for SSI checks. A regular bank account, such as a joint account between the child and parent, is not allowed. Only the representative—not the recipient—is supposed to have access to the funds in the account. This means that only the rep payee (not the recipient) can be authorized to sign checks.

There are also rules about the way an account must be titled. Both the rep payee's and the recipient's names must appear on the account. However, the title must show that the representative only has a fiduciary interest (not an ownership interest) in the account. Thus, the account can only be titled in either one of two ways:

- (Recipient's name) by (your name), representative payee
- (Your name), representative payee for (recipient)

The bank that you select can assist you to title the account. The instructions to do so are provided in the guidelines that Social Security issues to participating financial institutions.

Responsibilities

As rep payee, you must use the recipient's SSI funds only for his or her benefit. This means that you cannot spend the SSI benefits on yourself or other family members.

There are also record keeping requirements. You must keep track of how much money you receive and how much you spend and save. Your records should include bank statements, cancelled checks, the original check register, and receipts for all purchases you make.

If there is a large expenditure, such as a vacation for your son or daughter to visit family or friends, you could consider itemizing each individual expense. Some rep payees even keep detailed notes, including records of conversations, explaining why they thought a specific expenditure was a good idea.

Good record keeping is important because every year you must complete a Representative Payee Report for Social Security. In that report, you must document the amount of SSI funds you received in the past year and how you spent or saved them. There is a sample form (the "Representative Payee Report") on the Social Security website (http://www.ssa.gov).

Social Security sometimes asks the rep payee to bring the recipient's bank statements, income tax returns, and other records to the Social Security office. In that case, you will receive a written notice from Social Security specifying the date, time, and office where you need to appear.

Where to Learn More

To get official information about representative payment, you can read the Social Security publication, *A Guide for Representative Payees.* It is available on the Social Security website (http://www.ssa.gov) or by calling Social Security's main number (1-800-772-1213).

6

SSI Appeals

Topics include

Working with an attorney
Review by the local office
Hearing before an Administrative Law Judge
Appeals Council review
Federal Court

Sometimes SSI claims are denied. Despite your best efforts, you may not be able to persuade Social Security of the merits of your son's or daughter's case. In that event, you have the right to ask for the decision to be reviewed. Adverse decisions can be appealed through several stages of review within the Social Security system and, ultimately, in federal court.

Why Appeal?

It can often be worthwhile to appeal a denial of benefits. According to analysts, about half of all claims that were initially denied are eventually reversed. Therefore, you have about a fifty-fifty chance of winning on appeal.

The appeal process is relatively user-friendly. You can submit new evidence, such as a current medical evaluation or a doctor's letter, at almost any stage of the review process.

There can be a significant financial incentive to appeal. If the appeal is successful, Social Security will award retroactive benefits from the date the person would have received benefits. These benefits can sometimes amount to several thousand dollars.

Getting Legal Help

A person's chances of success on appeal can be vastly improved if they have an experienced attorney or advocate. These experts can provide many valuable services. They can review documents to spot flaws in the case, help obtain expert evaluations and reports, research and write legal briefs, and even argue the case to a judge.

Finding a lawyer

How can you find a qualified attorney? A good source of information is often the Social Security denial notice itself. The notice must include a list of resources that assist people with Social Security appeals, such as disability law groups, law schools, and legal aid organizations. There is also information in the Appendix.

How much do lawyers charge?

Many public advocacy organizations do not charge any fees for their services.

There are limits on the fees private attorneys can charge. The maximum fee is 25 percent of past due benefits, or $4,000, whichever is less. Past due benefits means the unpaid SSI benefits that accumulated while the appeal was being processed.

The attorney's fee must be approved by Social Security. In determining the appropriate fee, Social Security will consider, among other things, the background and skills of the attorney, the complexity of the case, the time involved, the result obtained, and—most important—whether you consent to the proposed fee.

Reconsideration

The first review stage is Reconsideration. The review process is different depending on whether the issue involves a disability-related issue or a non-disability issue.

- Reviews of disability-related issues are handled outside the Social Security office by reviewers who Social Security hires for this purpose. The applicant cannot participate directly in the review process. However, as I explain below, you should check the file and make sure it is reasonably complete before it is sent for review.

- Reviews of non-disability related issues are performed at the local office that denied the claim. However, the reviewer is a Social Security employee who was not involved in the initial decision. Non-disability issues would include disputes about amount of the applicant's resources, whether a UTMA account or trust is a countable resource, the person's earnings, living arrangement, or immigration status.

How to prepare a Request for Reconsideration

There are two ways to ask for an initial denial to be reconsidered. One way is to use the form provided by Social Security (form SSA-561-U2, "Request for Reconsideration"). This form is usually sent by Social Security with the denial notice. The form can also be obtained from any Social Security office or from the Social Security website (http://www.ssa.gov). The other way to request an appeal is simply to write a letter to Social Security stating that you are dissatisfied with the decision and want it reviewed.

Note that there are strict time limits for filing for Reconsideration. The appeal forms must be filed with Social Security within 60 days from the date the claimant receives the notice denying benefits.

To protect your appeal rights, be sure to document your actions. Make a photocopy of the signed paperwork for your records and then send the original documents to Social Security at the address provided in the denial notice. Be sure to use certified mail. Documents are sometimes lost or misplaced at Social Security.

Instead of mailing the appeal forms, you can deliver them to any local Social Security office. In the case of hand delivery, be sure to ask Social Security to date stamp your copy of the appeal form. That way, you will have proof that your appeal was properly filed.

Appeals of medical issues

If you are appealing Social Security's denial that your son or daughter has a disability, the review will be done by an outside firm that Social Security hires for this purpose. There will not be an appeal hearing at the local Social Security office. However, you can submit new documents that you want the reviewer to consider, such as a current medical report, vocational evaluation, or letter from a teacher.

Appeals of non-medical issues

Appeals of non-medical issues take place at the Social Security office where the matter was initially decided. Non-medical issues include things like the amount of resources, whether the applicant made an impermissible transfer of resources, and whether the amount of SSI is proper.

On the appeal form, there is a check-off-the-box section where you must choose one of three types of review. You can select a *case review, formal conference, or informal conference.* As I explain below, for most applicants, the *informal conference* will probably be sufficient.

- *Case review.* At a case review, Social Security will re-examine the records in the file and any new documents that you choose to submit. In most cases, however, the case review is unlikely to produce a positive result. This is because the case review is based on documents alone, and no actual hearing takes place. This means that you cannot present any testimony from live witnesses or argue the merits of the claim to the reviewer. Without your persuasive argument, the reviewer will probably not overturn the caseworker's decision, and the appeal will most likely be denied.
- *Formal conference.* For a *formal conference,* you can ask Social Security to send subpoenas (enforceable orders) to compel witnesses to appear and testify on the claimant's behalf. This tactic could prove useful if a crucial witness is unwilling or unable for employment reasons to attend the hearing.
- *Informal conference.* At an informal conference, you can you discuss the claim with an agency representative and present testimony from witnesses. If you do not need Social Security's subpoena power to prove your case (see above), the *informal conference* will probably be sufficient.

What to expect at the informal conference

The conference takes place at the local Social Security office where the application was processed. A case conference is quite informal. There are no courtroom-type procedures or rules. You sit at the examiner's desk and explain in your own words why you think the decision was wrong.

An examiner who was not involved in the initial denial conducts the proceedings. The conference is tape-recorded. Your son or daughter is not required to attend the meeting, although in some cases his or her presence could be helpful. The reviewer may ask you or the witnesses questions, and he or she may also ask you to return another time for a further interview.

When to expect a decision

You should receive a written decision within 60 days.

Administrative Review

If the request for reconsideration is denied, you can proceed to the next level of appeal, which is a formal hearing before an administrative law judge.

How to request a hearing

To request an administrative hearing, use Social Security form HA-501-U5 ("Request for Hearing Before an Administrative Law Judge"). After you fill in the form, either send it by certified mail or personally deliver it to the address on the form, making sure to get a receipt as proof of delivery. Note that this form must be delivered to Social Security within 60 days of the date you receive the reconsideration denial.

After your request has been filed, you will be notified of the date, time, and location where the hearing will take place. The notice will also tell you the name of the judge who been assigned to hear your case. Don't expect to have a hearing right away. Due to the current backlog of cases in the Boston office, it is not unusual for claimants to wait a year or more for a hearing.

Submitting new evidence

You can submit new evidence that you want the judge to consider, such as a recent medical report or current evaluation. At this stage of review, however, there are time limits for filing additional documents. To be certain that the judge will consider your new documentary evidence, Social Security should receive it no more than ten days after you file your request for a hearing.

Preparing for the hearing

You and your legal representative should prepare as thoroughly as possible for the hearing. In general, this means once again reviewing the entire case file, which at this point will have been transferred from the local Social Security office to the hearing location. When you review the file, make sure that any new documents you have submitted are included so that the judge will have the complete file.

If you plan to present testimony from witnesses, you should interview them and prepare them for the hearing. If a witness will not voluntarily attend the hearing, you can compel him or her to appear by issuing a subpoena.

What to expect at the hearing

In contrast to the Reconsideration hearing, which is quite informal, the administrative hearing is a relatively formal proceeding. The hearing is presided over by an administrative law judge and takes place in a small courtroom. The witnesses take an oath before they testify, and the proceedings are tape-recorded. A Social Security representative may be present to explain, from that agency's perspective, why the claim was denied.

There are no rigid rules for presenting evidence. In most cases, the judge will extend himself or herself to be fair and impartial. Most judges will consider any evidence that even remotely supports the claim. If you present testimony from witnesses, these witnesses will be allowed to testify in their own words. It is not uncommon for the judge to question the witnesses directly.

If you present any documentary evidence, these documents will be made part of the formal record and taken into account when the judge makes his or her decision. To be assured that a document will become part of the formal record, you should file it within ten days of the date you request administrative review.

When to expect a decision

After the hearing, the judge will issue a written decision of his or her findings. This decision, which is usually quite lengthy and detailed, explains the facts and law the judge relied on in reaching the decision.

If the claim is denied, you can proceed to the next stage of review, which is an appeal to the Appeals Council (discussed below).

If the claim is approved, the applicant will receive SSI benefits retroactive to the date that he or she first qualified for benefits. Expect to receive a check in about 60 days.

Appeals Council

If the administrative law judge denies the claim, you can ask to have that decision reviewed by the Appeals Council, which is located in the State of Virginia. It is extremely unusual for the Appeals Council to reverse an administrative law judge's decision. Nevertheless, review by the Appeals Council is a necessary step to advance to the next level of appeal, which is bringing a lawsuit in federal court.

At the review, the Appeals Council examines the entire file, including the tape recording of the administrative hearing and the judge's written findings. The Appeals Council will also consider any new documentary evidence that you choose to submit, even if that evidence was not made available to the administrative law judge. In that case, however, you must submit the new evidence with the notice of appeal document.

Occasionally, the Appeals Council will send the case back to the administrative law judge for a further hearing on a specific issue. On rare occasions, the Appeals Council will hold its own hearing. In that case, you or your representative will have to travel to the hearing, which will take place in Washington, D.C.

Federal Court

If the Appeals Council denies the claim, you can bring a lawsuit in the federal district court. The case must be filed within 60 days from the date you received the denial from the Appeals Council.

To bring a lawsuit, you will need the services of an attorney who is familiar with Social Security laws and federal court procedures.

These kinds of lawsuits are extremely difficult to win. One disadvantage is that unlike all previous stages of review, you cannot submit any new evidence to the federal court. A case is decided solely on the file that the Appeals Council considered.

To win your case in federal court, you must persuade the court that there are either factual errors in the administrative law judge's decision or that he or she misapplied the law. Either proposition is quite difficult to prove. The success rate is low.

Nevertheless, if you are successful, there can be a significant financial advantage to your son or daughter. In addition to qualifying for current monthly SSI benefits, he or she will collect a retroactive award of benefits. That award, which could easily go back several years to when he or she should have begun to receive benefits, could amount to tens of thousands of dollars.

Re-applying for Benefits

Instead of appealing to federal court, your son or daughter can file a new application if the circumstances have changed significantly since the prior application. In most cases, Social Security does not permit a person to file a new application while there is an appeal pending at any level. An exception would be if the basis for the new application is different from the issue that is being appealed.

7

Managing the SSI Benefit

Topics include

Overpayments
Representative payee liability
Useful strategies to avoid repaying SSI benefits
What can you use SSI benefits to pay for?

You have managed to get SSI for your son or daughter, and you might even be the representative payee. What do you do need to do now?

You owe it to your son or daughter to keep the SSI checks arriving regularly and to avoid any problems with Social Security. Above all, you want to steer clear of a situation where SSI benefits that were received in the past might have to be repaid. Avoiding repayment is for your own protection too, because you—the rep payee—could be asked to repay Social Security out of your personal funds.

Managing the SSI benefits is not really very difficult if you employ sound practices, especially good record keeping and reporting, and keep the assets below $2,000.

This section explains what you need to know to manage the SSI benefits effectively and avoid problems with Social Security.

Avoid Repaying SSI

One day, you open your mail from Social Security. Instead of an innocuous form letter, there is a legal notice demanding that your son or daughter must repay the agency thousands of dollars in past SSI benefits. How can this be? Social Security already made you come into the office and reprimanded you for letting the bank account go over $2,000. But you reduced the balance right away, and the agency seemed satisfied. Can this really be happening?

Social Security's right to repayment

Few things can be more anxiety provoking than getting an unexpected demand for a substantial sum of money from a large government agency. Yet it is not unusual for Social Security to claim that SSI recipients have been "overpaid" and must now repay benefits they previously received.

An overpayment can occur if a recipient inadvertently exceeds the asset or income limitations. These limits are firm and quite rigidly enforced by Social Security.

If a recipient accidentally allows his or her bank account to exceed the $2,000 limit in any particular month, any benefits received that month may be considered an overpayment. And if the account balance remains above $2,000 for a significant period of time, the overpayment demand can amount to thousands of dollars.

> John receives SSI of $704 per month. For ten months, his bank account contains about $3,000. Social Security can demand that John repay $7,040 (the entire monthly benefit for the ten month period the bank account exceeded $2,000).

An SSI recipient can also lose his current SSI benefit if the resources are not promptly reduced. In the above example, Social Security would probably send John a notice stopping his SSI payments because his resources have exceeded the $2,000 asset limit. John's benefits would not resume until he has $2,000 or less in resources.

In most overpayment cases, the recipient eventually ends up repaying Social Security, even after all the appeals have been exhausted. This is because the legal defenses to overpayments are quite limited. After all, the agency itself has written the rules on what defenses it will consider. Another reason is that the agency adheres to a rather strict "the rules are the rules" approach. The caseworkers have little discretion to bend the rules or even make judgment calls.

Keeping tabs on recipients

Before an overpayment situation can occur, Social Security has to find out that there has been a program violation. How do these missteps come to the agency's attention?

Not much gets by Social Security. If the recipient works, Social Security will contact the employer and make arrangements to receive the recipient's wage information electronically. Most banks will provide Social Security with the recipient's account balance every month.

All recipients (or their representatives) must periodically attend personal interviews at the local office. These meetings take place about every six months for wage earners and annually for most other recipients. The recipient is usually asked to bring all bank statements, W-2 forms, pay stubs, and any other financial records verifying income and resources.

Social Security also keeps tabs on recipients by routinely cross-checking information with the Internal Revenue Service. If there is a discrepancy between what the IRS records show and what the recipient has reported, Social Security may send out a notice of inquiry. This notice tells the recipient to appear at the local office and bring specific financial records. If the recipient does not have the records, he or she may be asked to sign a release that permits the agency to obtain the records directly from the financial institution or employer.

Appeals of Overpayments

A demand for repayment of SSI benefits can be appealed within the Social Security system. The first level of review is Reconsideration, which takes place at the local office level. If the Reconsideration decision is not favorable, you can request further review before an administrative law judge.[5]

On appeal, you can attempt to show that the agency is wrong and no overpayment occurred (if you believe that is the case). But even if you

---

5   Appeals of adverse decisions are discussed in Chapter 6, "SSI Appeals." There is also a detailed discussion of SSI appeals, including legal defenses, in *An Advocate's Guide to Surviving the SSI System*, listed in the Resources section.

admit that Social Security is correct and that benefits were overpaid, you can still ask Social Security to forgive ("waive") repayment.

Repaying SSI Benefits

Perhaps, at a hearing, you persuade Social Security of the merits of your claim. In that case, repayment will be waived. But if you choose not to appeal, or if the appeal is unsuccessful, Social Security must be repaid.

Repayment is made by reducing the current SSI benefit until restitution has been made in full. There are limits on how much current SSI can be reduced. SSI cannot be lowered more than 10 percent per month, no matter how great the overpayment. And in some cases, Social Security will voluntarily accept lower amounts—as little as $1 per month—until the balance has been repaid. No interest or penalty charges are ever imposed.

If the recipient no longer gets SSI and cannot repay Social Security in full right away, the agency will usually agree to an installment plan. The agency may also be willing to accept a compromise settlement. A compromise involves making a lump sum payment that is less than the full amount owed.

Representative payee's personal liability for an overpayment

Social Security sometimes demands that the rep payee reimburse the agency from his or her personal assets. This step is somewhat unusual, according to analysts. It could occur if the amount at issue is substantial *and* the situation that led to the overpayment was especially egregious. Some examples would be if the recipient—with the rep payee's knowledge—hid assets, or the rep payee used the recipient's resources for himself.

Useful Strategies

Obviously, instead of relying on Social Security to waive collection, it is better to avoid risking your son's or daughter's SSI benefit in the first place. Here are a few easy strategies you can employ.

Simplify

Consolidate all assets into one account, the rep payee's checking account. That way, there is only one asset to keep track of.

Follow good bookkeeping practices

Balance the checkbook on a monthly basis. Anticipate that SSI will be deposited on the first day of each month and plan accordingly. Some rep payees try to keep the maximum bank balance at or below $1,000. That way, there is some leeway if the recipient has few expenses in any particular month.

Use a debit card

To manage the bank account effectively, consider using a debit card to make purchases. With a debit card, the account balance is reduced right away without waiting for checks to clear. You can also use the debit card to withdraw cash if your son or daughter needs any cash on hand.

Promptly report any changes in income or resources

If there are any changes in your son's or daughter's financial circumstances that could affect the benefit amount, you should inform Social Security about them right away, in writing. If you call Social Security, be sure to follow up your conversation with a letter.

The changes you must report include any increase in income (such as wages) that would reduce the benefit. You must also report any additions to resources such as an inheritance or a substantial gift that puts the resource amount over $2,000.

You should promptly report any changes, ideally within ten calendar days, but no later than 30 days after the month in which the change occurred.

What Can You Use SSI to Pay For?

According to the Social Security Administration, you can spend

SSI on almost anything, as long as it is only for the recipient and does not benefit anyone else. SSI benefits should not be given away. An exception would be inexpensive gifts that the recipient gives to friends, family, and staff on holidays and other special occasions.

Here are some common items that SSI can be used to pay for:

Medical/health

Counseling
Evaluations
Insurance premiums and
    copayments
Special diet foods
Supplies and equipment
Therapies
Vitamins and supplements
Telephone, cell phone,
    internet charges
Utilities (gas, electric, heat, etc.)

Household items/items
for one's room

Dishes, utensils, kitchen supplies
Furniture
Decorative items
Household items
Linens

Recreation

Classes/instruction
Field trips
Health club membership
Leisure activities
One-to-one assistance
Summer camp

Housing expenses

Cable television
Cleaning supplies
Food
House cleaning
Landscaping, yard work
Laundry supplies
Live-in support staff
Paper products
Rent

Gifts

Gifts for family, friends, and staff

Transportation

Automobile expenses (gas,
    insurance, maintenance, etc.)
Subway passes
Tickets for The Ride

Education/vocational training

Classes
Job coach
Lessons
Travel between home and work
Tuition
Tutoring

Travel costs (including staff)
Vacations

Entertainment/Exercise

Bicycle/helmet
Camera
Computer
DVD player
Exercise bicycle
Music player/music
Skis/equipment
Television
Trampoline
Treadmill
Video games
Wii system and software

Personal Items

Books/books on tape
Clothing and accessories
Haircuts
Newspaper/magazines
Toiletries

These examples are just some of the ways that SSI benefits can be used to meet the recipient's ongoing needs and enrich the life of a person with a disability. But what if SSI is not enough? Parents may need to fill the gaps between what the government provides and what their children with disabilities need. How to do this without disrupting the flow of the SSI benefits is the subject of the next chapter.

8

Supplementing SSI

Topics include

Avoid paying for food and shelter
Three strategies that will not reduce SSI
Paying for medical care, housing,
recreation, and transportation

When a son or daughter with a disability leaves home, government programs may pay for some of their support. Still, government programs do not usually provide everything a person needs to live independently. That means that parents may still have to help. But how will your financial contribution affect SSI? Earlier, I explained how a recipient's benefit may be reduced if he or she gets any cash, food, or shelter. In this chapter, I explain three basic strategies you can use to help your son or daughter financially without risking SSI.

SSI and Independent Living

There are many state funded programs that help people with disabilities live independently from their families. If a person can live by himself in an apartment, there are rental subsidies that pay some of the rent directly to the landlord. If a person cannot live alone, some all-inclusive programs provide housing, meals, and 24-hour staff supervision.

These programs are not free of charge, however. A person who lives in a group home or similar living arrangement that is subsidized by the state must pay about 75 percent of monthly income as a program fee. Thus, a person who receives SSI of $704 per month (the SSI benefit for

53

a person who lives in a shared living arrangement) would pay about $528 per month to the agency. That would leave only about $176 per month for a personal allowance.

A person who lives in an apartment and receives a rental subsidy such as Section 8 must pay about 30 percent of gross income as rent. Thus, a person who gets SSI of $788 per month would pay about $236 per month in rent. This would leave only about $552 per month for utilities, food, travel between home and work, clothes, and recreation.

If your son or daughter does not get any government help, you might even have to pay for all his or her basic support costs, such as rent, utilities, food, and staff supervision.

Sending an Allowance is not the Answer

Helping a person who receives SSI financially is not as easy as sending a check every month. If you did that, you would be wasting your money, because if a person receives more than $20 per month in cash, SSI will be reduced on a dollar for dollar basis and could be eliminated altogether.

If a person gets any outside help with food or shelter, SSI could be reduced by up to about one-third of the monthly benefit amount ($244 per month in 2010). Chapter 2, "Qualifying for SSI," explains this rule.

But that does not mean you cannot help. It's just that with SSI, *how* you give can be as important as *how much* you give.

Three Useful Strategies

To avoid reducing SSI, follow these three strategies.

Strategy No. 1: Do not give your son or daughter any cash

Avoid giving any cash to your son or daughter who receives SSI. If a recipient gets more than $20 in cash in any month, SSI will be reduced dollar for dollar.

> John gets SSI and has no other income. His parents give him $100. John's SSI benefit for

that month will be reduced by $80. (The first $20 of unearned income is disregarded.)

While this rule may seem harsh in theory, its effect is not necessarily overly severe. This is because SSI counts income only on a month-to-month basis. If there is excess income in any one month, SSI is reduced only for that month. The next month's payment will not be affected.

In the above example, even if John received $2,500, he would only lose SSI for that month. The next month, he would receive the full SSI benefit. This assumes, of course, that John spent the $2,500 and did not retain it. If he kept the $2,500, he would have more than $2,000 in resources and could not get SSI until the resources were reduced to $2,000 or less.

Strategy No. 2: Avoid giving your son or daughter any food or shelter items

Perhaps your son or daughter lives with a roommate or in a group home. In that case, he or she is expected to pay for all food and shelter costs from the SSI stipend. (The items that Social Security defines as shelter-related are listed later in this chapter.) If an SSI recipient gets help with food or shelter items from an outside source, including his family, SSI will be reduced. The amount of the reduction is the item's actual value or one-third of the federal SSI benefit ($244 in 2010), whichever is less.

> Christine's parents buy her $100 worth of food. Christine's SSI benefit will be reduced by $80. (The first $20 of unearned income is disregarded.)

> Erica lives in her own apartment. One month, her parents pay her landlord $250. Erica's SSI benefit for that month will be reduced by $244. (The maximum reduction in any one month is $244.)

Fortunately, the monthly SSI benefit is never reduced by more than

$244 (in 2010), no matter how much you contribute. If, in the above example, Erica's parents paid her landlord $750, Erica's SSI benefit would still only be reduced by $244.

Strategy No. 3: Pay your son's or daughter's bills instead of giving him or her money to pay the bills

If your son or daughter incurs any bills, you should pay the creditor directly. That way, your son or daughter will be "out of the loop," and SSI will not be affected.

> Melanie, an SSI recipient, needs dental care costing $350. Melanie's mother pays the dentist directly. Melanie's SSI benefit is not affected. But if Melanie's mother gave Melanie $350 to pay the dentist, Melanie's SSI benefit would be reduced by $330 ($350 if Melanie had other unearned income).

Note, however, that the strategy of paying creditors directly will not work for food or shelter items. If you pay more than $20 in any month for either of those items, your son's or daughter's SSI benefit will be reduced.

> Richard has an overdue electric bill. His parents write a check for $175 payable to the utility company. That month, Richard's SSI is reduced by $175 ($155 if there is no other unearned income).

Supplementing SSI

Those are three ways that parents can use their own funds to supplement a son's or daughter's SSI benefit. Here are some ways to apply those strategies to real life situations.

Medical care

From an SSI perspective, there is generally no problem if you pay for medical care, since it does not involve food or shelter. You can safely pay for any items and services that are not covered by MassHealth or other insurance, such as premiums, co-payments, dental care, medications, vitamins, and supplements. Just be sure to pay the medical provider directly. Do *not* give your son or daughter money to pay the bill.

Transportation

If your son or daughter uses public transportation, you can purchase subway tokens, an MBTA pass, or tickets for The Ride directly from the MBTA. If your son or daughter uses specialized transportation and there is a fee for service, you can pay the vendor directly.

If your son or daughter owns an automobile, you can pay for gas, oil, insurance, maintenance, and inspections. But you should avoid giving cash to your son or daughter to pay for these car related items. Instead, you could obtain a gas credit card in your own name for him or her to use and then pay the bill from your personal funds. Make sure the card is never used for cash withdrawals or to buy food at the gas station.

Clothes

We want our children to look good. Fortunately, it is now possible to buy them clothes without causing a problem with SSI. Until 2005, if an SSI recipient received any clothes free of charge, the SSI benefit was reduced. That restriction has been eliminated.

Housing

If your son or daughter needs financial help with housing, it is quite difficult and probably impossible to avoid a reduction in SSI. The reason has to do with the high cost of housing in the greater Boston area. Under the SSI rules, if you contribute more than $20 per month toward rent, mortgage, utilities, or taxes, SSI will be reduced. And with apartments costing upwards of $1,200 per month, a $20 contribution will not go very far.

Still, with some creativity, you may be able to help.

First, let's start with a brief review of the housing rules. Not every housing-related expense causes a problem with SSI. Only the following ten items will reduce SSI:

- Mortgage (principal and interest)
- Rent
- Real estate taxes
- Gas
- Electricity
- Water
- Sewer
- Garbage removal
- Property insurance that is required by a lender
- Condominium charges that include any of the above items

If your son or daughter *rents* a home, he or she should pay for rent and utilities out of the SSI funds, if that is possible. You could pay for telephone, Internet access, cable television, and renter's insurance. You can also pay for non-food staple items such as paper products, laundry supplies, and cleaning items. You can also pay without penalty for any residential services your son or daughter needs to live independently. This could include salaries of live-in support staff or a personal assistant to help with tasks like hygiene, food shopping, cleaning, paying bills, banking, or budgeting.

What if your son or daughter *owns* a home, including a condominium? From the point of view of maximizing SSI, home ownership can present a challenge because of the high cost of real estate taxes. It can be quite difficult, if not impossible, for an SSI recipient to own a home without incurring a reduction in benefits.

Still, you can safely pay for telephone, Internet access, and cable television. You can also pay for landscaping, yard work, and snow removal. You can also pay for any repairs to the home and make capital improvements without affecting SSI. You can paint the house, repair the roof, update the kitchen and bath, add a ramp, or make other accessibility modifications without reducing SSI.

But despite your strategizing, maybe you can't avoid a reduction in SSI. In that case, you could take a glass-half-full approach. If you can afford to do so, why not pay most or all of the housing costs yourself? You could purchase a house or condominium (or a share of one) and pay for the mortgage, taxes, insurance, and utilities out of your personal funds. The property might be a good long-term investment. No matter how much you spend, SSI will not be reduced by more than $244 per month (in 2010).

Food

Getting outside help with food is also prohibited, according to the Social Security rules. One exception is food stamps, which an SSI recipient can receive without penalty. The current maximum food stamp benefit for one person is $200 per month (in 2010).

If your son or daughter likes to eat out, you can give him or her up to $20 per month plus another $20 per calendar quarter without causing a problem with SSI.

Recreation

You can pay items such as lessons, classes, and special events by giving money directly to the vendor. If you son or daughter wants movie passes or concert tickets, buy them from your personal funds and give them as a gift.

Vacations

To pay for your son's or daughter's vacation, give money directly to the travel agent or vendor. Vacations are one instance where you do not have to worry about the troublesome no-food-or-shelter rule. Social Security disregards those two items when a person receives them away from home, such as on a vacation.

9

Work and SSI

Topics include

Student earnings
Adult earnings
Work related expenses

When an SSI recipient gets a job, his earnings can work against him for SSI purposes. In general, as earnings increase, SSI benefits go down and may stop altogether if earnings are too high.

This is logical, because SSI is a program for people with disabilities who are unable to be "gainfully employed." In judging whether a person can perform gainful employment, Social Security uses an earnings test. As a general rule, if a person can earn more than $1,000 per month in 2010 ($1,640 if blind), then he or she is presumed to be capable of gainful employment and cannot get SSI.

This rule has several exceptions, however, and in fact many SSI recipients earn more than $1,000 per month. This is because Social Security has enacted several "work incentive" programs that allow recipients to work and still collect SSI.

The work incentive programs covered in this chapter are Excluded Student Earnings; the Earned Income Exclusion; Impairment-Related Work Expenses (IRWE); and the PASS.

The Resources section also contains some helpful publications and websites on employment related topics.

Excluded Student Earnings

If an SSI recipient is under age 22 and regularly attends school, Social Security will exclude up to $1,640 of earnings per month (up to a maximum of $6,600 per calendar year) in 2010. For SSI purposes, "regularly attending school" means that a person takes one or more courses of study and attends classes:

- In a college or university for at least eight hours a week; or
- In grades 7-12 for at least 12 hours a week; or
- In a training course to prepare for employment for at least twelve hours a week (15 hours a week if the course involves "shop" practice); or
- For less time than indicated above for reasons beyond the student's control, such as illness.

> Sean, who is age 19 and a special education student, works on Saturdays at an auto body shop. He earns $70 per week, and in 2010 he earns $3,000 from this source. Since $3,000 is below the $6,600 amount Social Security disregards, Sean's SSI benefit is not affected.

Earned Income Exclusion

Social Security does not count the first $65 of a recipient's monthly earnings. Also, one-half of what is earned over $65 per month is not counted.

> Sharon, age 25, earns $430 per month from a part-time job and has no other income besides SSI of $788 per month.

$430	earned income
-20	SSI General Exclusion ($20)
$410	
-65	SSI earned income disregard ($65)

$345
-172   one-half of remaining earned income
$173   countable earned income

$788   maximum SSI benefit
-173   less countable income
$615   reduced SSI benefit

Sharon has $1,045 per month available for her self-support (earnings of $430 plus SSI of $615).

Impairment-Related Work Expenses

If a person needs special items or services in order to work, they can be deducted from the person's earnings when SSI is calculated. This is true even if the items and services are also needed for normal daily activities. Some examples of Impairment-Related Work Expenses (IRWE) include:

- Accessibility modifications to a residence
- Attendant care services
- Equipment, such as a wheelchair
- Guide dog
- Medical devices and supplies

To qualify as an IRWE, the item or service must be directly related to the person's work. If a person also uses the item or service in normal daily activities, then only the work-related portion of the cost qualifies. For example, a person who works might need an attendant every day to help get her get up, dress, bathe, and go to work. The attendant's services on workdays would be deductible, but not on non-work days.

An important point about IRWE is that to be deductible, the item or service must be paid for by the person himself, as opposed to his or her insurance or a third party. So if the worker's family paid for a special transportation item, the payment would not be allowed as an IRWE.

The following example illustrates how an IRWE can offset income, allowing a person to increase his aggregate income from earnings and SSI.

> Frank earns $650 per month in supported employment and has no other income. His IRWE is $250 per month. The maximum SSI benefit for his category is $788 per month.

$650	earned income
-20	SSI General Exclusion ($20)
$630	remaining earned income
-65	SSI earned income disregard ($65)
$565	remaining earned income
-250	less IRWE
$315	remaining earned income
-157	one-half of remaining earned income
$158	countable earned income
$788	maximum SSI benefit
-158	less countable earned income
$630	reduced SSI benefit

> Frank has $1,030 per month available for his self-support. You arrive at this amount by subtracting the IRWE of $250 from gross earnings of $650 ($650 - $250 = $400) and then adding SSI of $630 ($400 + $630 = $1,030).

Plan To Achieve Self-Support (PASS)

A PASS is a way that a person with a disability can set aside either income or resources, or both, while working toward an occupational goal. While a PASS is in place, a person can earn more income and retain more resources than would ordinarily be the case with SSI.

Social Security must approve a PASS before it can be put into place. Also, there are some guidelines that must be followed. A PASS must:

- Be designed specifically for the person's own needs, goals, abilities, and other circumstances
- Be in writing and signed by the person for whom it is written
- Have a designated and feasible work goal that states the person's proposed job, that he or she has a reasonable chance of getting and keeping the job, and will earn additional income that is enough to achieve self-support
- Have a timetable for achieving the goal (the initial period cannot exceed 18 months, but with extensions, the PASS can continue for 48 months total)
- Show what income and resources the person has and will receive that will be used to achieve the work goal, and how the income and resources will be used
- Show how the money set aside for resources will be kept identifiable from other money the person owns

The following example shows how a PASS can benefit a person who wants to become self-supporting.

> Maria, who receives SSI of $704 per month, is taking courses to become a lab assistant, with the goal of becoming self-supporting. During an internship, her salary will be $1,200 per month. She will have monthly expenses of $450 for child care and transportation. By using a PASS, Maria can collect the full SSI benefit during her internship. Without a PASS, Social Security would reduce Maria's benefit during her internship. The following shows the calculation:

| $1,200 | earned income |
| -20 | SSI General Exclusion ($20) |

| $1,180 | remaining earned income |
| -65 | SSI earned income disregard ($65) |

$1,115   remaining earned income
-557   less one-half of remaining earned income
$558   countable earned income

$704   SSI benefit
-558   less countable earned income
$146   reduced SSI benefit

Comparison of Benefits

	Not Working	Working without PASS	Working with PASS
Income	0		
Salary	0	$1,200	$1,200
SSI	$704	$146	$704
	$704	**$1,346**	**$1,904**
Expenses			
Child Care and Transportation	0	$450	$450
Net income	**$704**	**$896**	**$1,454**

10

SSDI, Medicare, Medicaid, and Related Programs

Topics include

Social Security Disability Insurance (SSDI)
Medicare
MassHealth
Adult Family Care Program
Personal Care Attendant Program

Besides SSI, there are other public benefit programs that support people with disabilities. The programs discussed in this chapter are Social Security Disability, Medicare, and Medicaid (called MassHealth in Massachusetts). Two MassHealth Programs that pay caregivers to provide personal care to a person with a disability are Adult Family Care and the Personal Care Attendant Program.

Social Security Disability Insurance (SSDI)

General program description

If a person has worked and paid into the Social Security system, his or her son or daughter with a disability may be able to receive SSDI. Compared to SSI, the SSDI program rules are much more manageable:

- The SSDI benefit amounts are usually higher than for SSI.
- There is no asset limit. A recipient can own significant assets and still receive benefits.

- The work rules are more lenient under the SSDI program. Unlike SSI benefits, which can fluctuate from month to month depending on a person's earnings, the SSDI benefit amount remains constant.

But there is a downside too. Unlike SSI, there is no automatic MassHealth entitlement. A person who needs MassHealth must qualify under the state program rules. These rules are discussed later in this chapter.

A person cannot "opt out" of SSDI in order to collect SSI/Medicaid. When a person applies for benefits, Social Security will assess entitlement for both programs. If the person qualifies for SSDI, that program will be primary. Some people receive benefits under both SSI and SSDI. This is explained later in this chapter.

Who can get benefits?

There are three ways and person can qualify for SSDI benefits:

- A worker who becomes medically disabled can collect benefits based on his or her own work record. To qualify, a person must not be working (or, if working, earn less than $1,000 per month in 2010). A person must also have worked a sufficient number of quarters of "covered" employment before becoming disabled. In general, that means one must have accrued 20 quarters of employment that were earned in the last 10 years ending with the year the disability began.
- A minor (under age 18) dependent of a disabled, retired, or deceased worker can collect benefits up through age 18, or through age 19 if enrolled in school.
- The disabled son or daughter of a disabled, retired, or deceased worker can get benefits for life.[6] To qualify, the son's or daughter's disability must have started before age 22 and remained continuous through the time he or she is claiming benefits.

---

6   A disabled son or daughter who is age 18 or older is called a "disabled adult child," or DAC.

> Jonathan, who is age 25 and has developmental disabilities, can collect SSDI benefits, based on his father's work record when his father begins to draw benefits.

> Melissa, who becomes disabled at age 25 due to a car accident, cannot get SSDI benefits based on her parent's work record because she has not been continuously disabled since before age 22.

Benefit amounts

A disabled dependent's SSDI award is based on his or her parent's benefit. That benefit is set according to the parent's earnings record. In most cases, a disabled dependent receives 50 percent of the parent's benefit while the parent is living and 75 percent of the benefit after the parent has died.

These amounts are subject to a "Family Maximum Benefit" that Social Security establishes for the insured worker. Under this formula, if a disabled, retired, or deceased worker has dependent family members, the total benefits payable to both the worker and the family members may not exceed a Family Maximum Benefit established by Social Security. The worker is paid first, and the worker's benefit is not reduced by any dependent's benefits that may be paid on his or her record.

Recipients of both SSI and SSDI ("Dual Recipients")

Some recipients can get both SSDI and SSI concurrently. This might occur if the SSDI amount is lower than the maximum SSI benefit for the person's category. In that case, the person's combined SSDI and SSI benefit must equal the maximum SSI benefit for the person's category.

> Robert, who lives independently, is receiving SSI benefits of $704 per month. Then his father retires and Robert becomes entitled to receive $500 of SSDI benefits based on his father's work

record. Robert's SSI benefit will be reduced by $480 due to the income from SSDI. (Social Security disregards $20 of SSDI income and counts $480. $500 - $20 = $480.) Robert will receive $224 in SSI benefits ($704 - $480 = $224). Robert will receive $724 in combined SSDI and SSD benefits (SSDI of $500 + SSI of $224 = $724).

Comparison of SSI and SSDI

	SSI	SSDI
Asset limit	Yes	No
Limit on earned income	Yes	Yes*
Limit on unearned income	Yes	No
Benefit can fluctuate each month	Yes**	No
Entitlement based on financial need	Yes	No
Automatic Medicare entitlement	No	Yes***
Automatic Medicaid entitlement	Yes	No

* If more than $1,000/month earned income in 2010
** If there is any earned or unearned income
*** After receiving SSDI for 24 months

SSDI and assets

Unlike SSI, there is no asset limit for the SSDI program. A person can have significant assets and still receive SSDI.

That can raise a question: If a person can own substantial assets directly in his or her own name and still receive SSDI, do the assets need to be protected in a special needs trust? Asked another way, why bother with the restrictions of a special needs trust if that kind of trust is not needed to receive SSDI?

Besides qualifying for public benefits, there may be other valid reasons that a special needs trust is a good idea. A special needs trust can assure sound financial management and prevent loss. Even if the SSDI program does not have any asset limits, other public benefit programs may have such restrictions. One example is MassHealth (Medicaid), which has a $2,000 asset cap for recipients age 65 and older.

SSDI and unearned income

The SSDI program does not consider any unearned income the individual receives. A person could have income from an annuity, rental property, or investment account without affecting SSDI.

SSDI and Medicare

SSDI recipients can get Medicare after they have qualified for SSDI for 24 months. The Medicare program is discussed later in this chapter. Note SSDI recipients—unlike SSI recipients—do not automatically qualify for MassHealth benefits.

SSDI and work

Earnings from employment and self-employment are treated differently under the SSDI program than they are under the SSI program. With SSI, a person's benefit can fluctuate every month depending on the amount of earnings. However, SSDI remains constant if the person earns less than $1,000 per month (in 2010).[7] If a person earns more than that amount, SSDI may end altogether. Another important point is that SSDI is never partially reduced. A recipient gets either the entire check or none at all.

> Robert gets SSDI of $895 per month based on his retired father's earnings, and he has earnings of $750 per month from a part-time job. Robert can keep all his earnings, because $750 is below the $1,000 per month earnings threshold amount.

> But if Robert earned $1,000 per month, he could lose SSDI altogether. This is because he has exceeded the earnings limit of $1,000 per month and is presumed to be capable of self-support.

Fortunately, Social Security has enacted several "work incentive" programs that may allow a person to earn more than $1,000 per month and still get SSDI. These include Impairment-Related Work Incentives (discussed in Chapter 9, "Work and SSI"), the Trial Work Period, and the Extended Period of Eligibility. Some important work incentives are only for SSDI recipients and others specifically assist blind recipients. A good source of information on these programs is Social Security's *Red Book on Employment* (listed in the Resources Section).

Medicare

Medicare is a federally funded medical insurance program. People who have qualified for SSDI for 24 months can get Medicare for themselves and their dependents. Social Security retirees can also receive Medicare as part of their retirement benefit.

---

7    $1,000 per month is a measure of a non-blind person's ability to perform substantial gainful activity (SGA). Chapter 9, "Work and SSI," discusses SGA. There is no SGA threshold for blind individuals who receive SSDI.

Medicare has several parts. This chapter explains parts A, B, C, and D.

Medicare Part A

Medicare Part A covers charges for a semi-private hospital room and board up to 60 days, subject to an annual deductible ($1,100 in 2010). For stays that last between 61 and 90 days, recipients pay co-insurance of $275 per day; and for stays between 91 and 150 days, recipients pay $550 per day. Medicare does not pay for stays longer than 150 days.

Medicare Part A also covers 20 days of skilled nursing care in a facility such as a rehabilitation hospital or a nursing home that has been approved by Medicare. After 20 days, recipients must pay coinsurance ($137.50 per day in 2010). After 100 days, Medicare will not pay for any care in a skilled care facility.

For most recipients, part A is free. However, because of the high cost of co-insurance payments, recipients should consider purchasing supplemental (Medigap) insurance.

Medicare Part B

Medicare Part B pays for physician services, hospital outpatient care, lab services, medical equipment, psychiatric care, physical and occupational therapy, and some preventative services.

The standard premium for Medicare B is $110.50 per month in 2010. However, not all recipients will pay this amount.

- Recipients who have the Medicare B premium deducted from their government benefit check will pay $96.40 for coverage. This is because in 2010, there is no cost-of-living adjustment to Social Security. Since recipients are protected from having their Social Security benefits decrease, these people will continue to pay the 2009 rate ($96.40 per month).
- Some recipients will pay a higher premium based on their annual earnings. For example, a single recipient with annual income between $85,001 and $107,000 (or a member of a couple

with income from $170,001 to $214,000) will pay $154.70 per month.

- Recipients who enrolled late or withdrew from the program and later re-enrolled will pay more than the standard premium. The amount of the premium will depend on several factors, including the date of enrollment.

There is an annual deductible of $155 for all Part B services.

In Massachusetts, Medicare recipients with very low income and few assets can qualify for state assistance in paying the Medicare B premium.

If the recipient does not elect Medicare Part C (discussed below), Medicare determines an allowable charge (the "approved amount") for Part B services and pays 80 percent of that amount. The remaining 20 percent is paid by recipients.

Medicare Part C

Medicare Part C, also called Medicaid Advantage, is Medicare's version of managed care. Medicare pays doctors and other medical providers who join the plan a fixed amount of money each year to manage the participant's care. Participants enroll with a private health insurance plan (Tufts, Blue Cross/Blue Shield, etc.). Participants may be restricted to using doctors in the plan's network. In exchange for this limitation, participants may get additional benefits such as extra days in the hospital and coverage for some prescription drugs. Each Medicare Advantage Plan sets its own terms, conditions, and costs.

Medicare Part D

Medicare Part D is the prescription drug benefit. Prescription drug coverage is available to anyone who is enrolled in Medicare. Medicare Part D is run through private drug plans known as Prescription Drug Plans (PDPs). Currently Massachusetts has 14 different PDPs, which each have their own coverage, terms, premiums, and deductible amounts.

Medicare drug plans have a "coverage gap," which is sometimes referred to as the "donut hole." A coverage gap means that after the member has spent a certain amount of money for drugs (no more than $3,850), he or she must pay for all drug costs while in the "gap." The maximum the person must pay while in the coverage gap is $3,052. Once the member has reached the plan's out of pocket limit, the person only has to pay a co-insurance amount (about 5 percent of the drug cost) or a co-payment for the rest of the calendar year. The co-payments are set by each PDP.

People who receive their prescription drug coverage through MassHealth must enroll in Medicare Part D. The Medicare Part D program will pay for drug costs, and MassHealth will pay for co-payments, deductibles, and the coverage gap.

Medicaid (MassHealth)

Medicaid, which is called MassHealth in Massachusetts, is a comprehensive medical insurance program for people who are poor or have disabilities. In Massachusetts, there are seven different MassHealth program types. This book covers two of these programs—MassHealth Standard and CommonHealth. Most individuals with disabilities receive benefits under one of these two programs. Information about all seven MassHealth program types is available on the MassHealth website (http://www.mass.gov.dma). MassHealth publishes a helpful booklet that you can obtain online or by calling the MassHealth customer service number (1-800-232-1340).

Overview of MassHealth Standard and CommonHealth

There are different eligibility rules for MassHealth Standard and CommonHealth depending on one's income, work status, and age (under age 65 or age 65 and over). Despite the differences in eligibility rules, the benefits provided under the two programs are almost identical. If a person must qualify for Medicaid in order to receive certain state-funded residential or employment services, participation in either MassHealth Standard or CommonHealth will satisfy the eligibility requirement.

What medical services do MassHealth Standard and CommonHealth pay for?

Covered services include hospital care, outpatient services, durable medical equipment, doctor visits, mental health services, and personal care attendant (PCA) services. MassHealth also pays for prescription drugs for individuals who do not receive Medicare D. (Individuals who receive Medicare must enroll in the Medicare D program. This is explained earlier in this chapter.)

Qualifying for MassHealth without SSI

SSI recipients automatically receive MassHealth Standard free of charge as a benefit of SSI. If a person with a disability does not receive SSI, it is possible to qualify separately for MassHealth.

MassHealth Standard

To qualify for MassHealth Standard, a person who is age 19 through 64 must have gross monthly income from all sources of no more than $1,201 for a single individual, or $1,457 for a couple (this is 133 percent of the Federal Poverty Level in 2010). There is currently no asset limit for persons under age 65. There is no premium for this program.

CommonHealth

For individuals ages 19 through 64, the CommonHealth rules are different depending on whether one is working or not working. Children ages 0 through 18 with disabilities can qualify for benefits by paying a monthly premium that is based on family income.

CommonHealth for working persons

If a person is working, he or she can qualify by paying a monthly premium, which is set on a sliding scale according to one's income. "Working" is defined as being employed an average of 40 hours or more per month, or 10 or more hours per week. If a person is employed fewer than 40 hours per month, the person must have worked at least

240 hours in the six months preceding application for benefits. The rate of pay is unimportant; a person who is earning as little as $1 per hour in a sheltered workshop can meet the work requirement.

CommonHealth for non-working persons

A person who is not working must meet a "one-time deductible" amount. This is the amount of medical bills a person must incur before he or she can qualify for MassHealth. A person who has paid the deductible amount can continue to receive MassHealth through age 65 (assuming that he or she still has a disability). There may be a small monthly premium depending on the person's income. Here is an example of how MassHealth would calculate the one-time deductible.

> Rachael, who is unmarried, receives gross SSDI of $1,200 per month (before the Medicare B premium is deducted). She has no other income. Her one-time deductible amount is computed as follows:

$1,300 per month	Income
-542	Income standard for family of one (figure is set by MassHealth)
$758	Balance
x6	
$4,548	Deductible amount

> In order to qualify for CommonHealth, Rachael must pay medical bills of $4,548 that are not covered by any other medical insurance. The medical bills that can be used include any unpaid medical bills (regardless of when they were incurred); medical bills incurred within the six-month period specified by MassHealth; modifications to a residence to make it accessible, adapted equipment (including a vehicle), and medical insurance premiums.

Children under age 19

Children under age 19 can qualify for MassHealth by paying a monthly premium. The premium is set on a sliding scale according to the family's income.

No asset limit

There is currently no asset limit for CommonHealth for persons under age 65.

Adult Family Care Program

The Adult Family Care program is known by several names. It is sometimes called Adult Foster Care, Adult Family Care, and Enhanced Family Care. The program pays a caregiver—including a parent—to provide services for a person with a disability who lives with the caregiver. The program rules are located at 130 C.M.R. 408.000. (CMR stands for the Code of Massachusetts Regulations.)[8]

How a person with a disability can qualify

Adult Family Care is a MassHealth program. The person who needs care must receive either MassHealth Standard or CommonHealth. In Massachusetts, people who receive SSI automatically get MassHealth. A person with a disability who does not receive SSI can enroll separately for MassHealth. There are instructions on how to do so in the MassHealth section of this chapter.

To qualify for the Adult Family Care program, a person must need help with at least one so-called activity of daily living (ADL). This could include bathing, getting dressed, using the toilet, transferring, ambulating, or eating. The person can qualify if he or she just needs supervision with these activities.

---

8   The Code of Massachusetts Regulations can be found online at http://www.lawlib.state.ma.us/source/mass/cmr/index.html.

Payment amounts

Adult Family Care currently has two levels of compensation for caregivers:

- If the person who needs care can be left alone for a brief period of time (about 15 minutes), the maximum rate is $19 per day.
- If the person cannot be left alone at all, the daily rate is $50, up to a maximum of $1,500 per month or $18,000 per year.

The income is free from federal and state income taxes.

A legal guardian may not be the paid caregiver

The state will not pay the person's spouse, parent (if the person who needs care is under age 18), or legal guardian to provide care. Therefore, if you are your son's or daughter's legal guardian and want to be the paid caregiver, you must resign as the guardian. If you are not already the guardian, you should consider not becoming the guardian if another family member (your spouse or child) can fill that role. Chapter 13, "Legal Requirements to Obtain Guardianship," discusses this topic.

Where to apply

You apply for the Adult Family Care Program through the Aging Service Access Point (ASAP) that covers your city or town. There are 31 ASAPs located throughout the state. Not every ASAP offers the program, so you may be referred to an agency that provides the service. To locate the ASAP that covers your city or town, call 1-800-AGEINFO or go to the website (http://www.800ageinfo.com). There is also a list of all the ASAPs in the Appendix.

Personal Care Attendant Program

The Personal Care Attendant (PCA) Program assists a person with a disability to hire caregivers to provide hands on physical assistance.

The person with a disability must live in his or her own home. The person hires, trains, schedules, and supervises the caregivers.

How a person with a disability can qualify

The PCA Program is part of MassHealth. To qualify, a person must receive either MassHealth Standard or CommonHealth. In Massachusetts, people who receive SSI automatically get MassHealth. A person with a disability who does not receive SSI can enroll separately for MassHealth. There are instructions on how to do this in Chapter 10, "SSDI, Medicare, MassHealth, and Related Programs." A person who is approved for MassHealth must qualify separately for the PCA program.

In addition to qualifying for MassHealth, a person must need hands-on assistance with at least two of seven ADLs: mobility, bathing/grooming, dressing/undressing, passive range-of-motion exercises, taking medications, eating, and toileting. After the PCA is hired, he or she can assist with activities such as laundry, shopping, light housekeeping, meal preparation, transportation to medical providers, and other special needs.

There is a separate application for the PCA program. The person must apply through one of the 29 Personal Care Management (PCM) agencies that evaluate MassHealth recipients for PCA care. You can locate a PCM agency by calling MassHealth customer service at 800-841-2900. There is also a list in the PCA Handbook, which is available through the Executive Office of Human Services website (http://www.mass.gov/eohhs).

Payment amounts

The Personal Care Attendant program pays caregivers based on an hourly rate, which is currently $11.60 (in 2010). The rate of payment will gradually increase to $12.48 per hour over the next two years.

A legal guardian may not be the paid caregiver

The PCA program will not pay a person's spouse, parent (if the person is under age 18), or legal guardian to be the caregiver. Thus, if you want to be the paid caregiver and you are already the legal guardian, you must resign. If you are not the legal guardian, you must find another family member to serve as the guardian.

Part II: Guardianship

EVER SINCE YOUR CHILDREN WERE BORN, you have had the right to speak for them. You sign their school permission slips, medical consents, and education plans. If "parental permission" is ever required to go on a field trip or enroll in summer camp, you simply sign your name.

But when your children reach age 18—legal adulthood in Massachusetts—that all changes.

Medical care, for example. If your adult son or daughter needs a particular medical procedure, your permission is no longer sufficient. He or she must personally give approval. But what if your son or daughter has a cognitive disability and cannot understand the treatment that is being proposed? A doctor might not be willing to provide care.

Even getting access to an adult son's or daughter's medical information can be problematic. Under the strict medical privacy laws (HIPPA), a healthcare provider is not supposed to disclose an adult patient's private medical information—even to immediate family members—without the patient's prior approval. What if your son or daughter does not give approval? You could be completely shut out of the medical information loop.

In the education arena, adult students with disabilities have the right to decide their own special education services. This means that your 18-year-old could decide to graduate with his or her class and forfeit future special education services. What would you do then?

Signing legal documents can be an issue too. In Massachusetts, an 18-year-old can legally sign—and be bound by—important legal documents such as leases, contracts, and credit card agreements. This can be true even if the person lacks the cognitive ability to understand the basic elements of what he or she is signing.

If any of this concerns you, then you should consider becoming your son's or daughter's legal guardian. As the legal guardian, you can take over decision making in important areas like as education, medical care, work, living arrangements, and finances.

This section explains what you need to know about becoming your son's or daughter's legal guardian. The topics include how to make the decision, some common alternatives to guardianship, and the guardian's responsibilities. I also discuss whether you should get legal help or do the legal work yourself.

Last, a new guardianship law—The Massachusetts Uniform Probate Code—took effect July 1, 2009. The MUPC changed much of the guardianship terminology and many of the forms. There are also new reporting requirements for guardians—including guardians who were appointed before July 1, 2009. The book covers the MUPC requirements.

11

Guardianship Basics

Topics Include

What is guardianship?
Deciding whether guardianship is necessary

What is Guardianship?

Guardianship is a court-ordered arrangement in which one person is given the legal authority to make decisions on behalf of another person whom a court has deemed to be "incapacitated." The guardian's decision-making authority extends to all areas specified by the court.

Under the new Massachusetts guardianship law that went into effect on July 1, 2009, there can be a *limited guardian* or a *general guardian*. A *conservator* manages the finances of a person with a disability. [9]

- A *limited guardian* makes decisions in only some specific areas, such as medical care. Limited guardianship may be appropriate if the person with a disability can make some decisions on his or her own.
- A *general guardian* has broad control and decision-making authority. General guardianship may be appropriate if the person has a significant intellectual disability or mental illness and, as

---

9   The new guardianship and conservatorship laws are part of the Massachusetts Uniform Probate Code, which is located at Massachusetts General Laws, chapter 190B. The guardianship provisions are contained in sections 5-301 to 5-313. The conservatorship provisions are contained in sections 5-401 to 5-431. The Uniform Probate Code can be located at any law library or online at www.mass.gov/legis/laws/mgl.

a result, is unable to meaningfully participate in important decisions that affect him or her.

- A *conservator* manages the finances (income and assets) of a person with a disability. A conservator has no authority to make personal decisions (medical, educational, etc.) for the person whose funds he or she is managing.

A person can be both a legal guardian and a conservator.

The different kinds of guardianship are discussed in more detail in Chapter 14, "Legal Requirements to Obtain Guardianship." Conservatorship is explained in Chapter 18, "Conservatorship."

Deciding Whether Guardianship is Necessary

For parents, the decision to seek guardianship can be difficult. You need to protect your son or daughter with a disability, but there may be some areas where he or she can make sound decisions. Fortunately, legal guardianship is not an "all or nothing" proposition. It is possible to carve out some areas where you son or daughter can retain important decision-making rights and control of his or her own life.

When considering how much authority you need—and how much independence your son or daughter should retain—begin with an assessment of the different areas where your son or daughter may need your assistance. These include medical, educational, financial, vocational/adult services, living arrangements, legal, self-care, safety, and communication. For each area, assess whether your son or daughter can do the following:

- Medical

  o Seek medical care when he or she is sick or injured
  o Weigh the risks and benefits of any particular medical procedure that is being proposed
  o Understand the need for routine medical care
  o Understand that even if a medical procedure is painful or unpleasant, it may still be necessary
  o Assess whether a particular medication is desirable, even though it may have unpleasant side effects

- o Provide accurate information about his or her medical condition
- o Follow medical advice

- Education

  - o Grasp the essentials of his or her learning problems and understand the services needed to learn effectively
  - o Advocate for himself or herself to obtain necessary education services

- Finances

  - o Understand money basics, including the purpose of money, how to count money, and how to make change
  - o Safeguard his or her money so that it is not lost or stolen
  - o Budget money so that some funds are available to pay expenses at the end of the month

- Vocational/adult services

  - o Apply for services from the Department of Disability Services, Department of Mental Health, or Massachusetts Rehab Commission, or other agency that serves people with disabilities
  - o Access necessary services and supports such as job training, employment support, or a day habilitation program
  - o Negotiate with the agency overseeing his or her care to obtain the best possible services

- Living arrangements

  - o Provide for his or her own physical care and well-being such as purchasing proper food, clothing, and shelter
  - o Live harmoniously in a group setting, respecting others' needs for quiet, privacy, and cleanliness

- Legal and decision-making

  o Understand the implications of signing documents
  o Make sound decisions in important areas such as living arrangements, school, and work

- Self-care and safety

  o Have personal safety skills, such as staying out of dangerous areas, not talking to strangers, and keeping doors locked
  o Know how to summon help in an emergency such as a fire or accident
  o Have basic safety skills such as being careful around fires, stoves, candles, etc.

- Communication

  o Communicate effectively (verbally or by other means)
  o Understand that he or she has choices and be able to express them

Even if your son or daughter needs help with any of the above items, you should also consider whether he or she could be assisted by any means short of guardianship. For example, sometimes a person who needs help to make medical decisions can appoint a health care agent to act on his or her behalf. A person who receives government benefits such as Supplemental Security Income (SSI) or Social Security Disability Insurance (SSDI) can have a representative payee manage them. The "less restrictive alternatives" to guardianship are covered in the next chapter. Chapter 17, "Financial Management," discusses alternatives to conservatorship that do not require court involvement.

12

Alternatives to Guardianship

Topics include

Health care proxy
Medical release
Durable power of attorney

To approve a guardianship, a Court must be persuaded that there are no "less restrictive alternatives" to guardianship. You must prove to the Court's satisfaction that your son's or daughter's interests cannot be adequately protected by any less intrusive, voluntary arrangements. This chapter covers some common alternatives to guardianship.

Note that most of the arrangements discussed in this chapter require a person to be legally competent. This means that the person must have sufficient cognitive ability to understand the document he or she is being asked to sign. If your son or daughter is cognitively challenged or mentally ill to the degree that he or she cannot comprehend, at least in a general way, the arrangement that is being proposed, guardianship may be necessary.

Another important point is that all the arrangements are voluntary and can be terminated at will by the person who agreed to them. Your control may be illusory. Your son or daughter can withdraw consent at any time and nullify the arrangement.

Release and Authorization for Medical Information

To make sure you can get basic information about your son's or daughter's medical care, he or she can sign a medical release form. That form will allow you to get your son's or daughter's private medical

91

records directly from third parties. If you have any questions about treatment, you can discuss them with the healthcare provider.

This arrangement has some limitations:

- In most cases, the release form must be directed to a specific health care provider and identify the kind of medical information being requested. It cannot usually be open ended.
- The release form only authorizes you to talk to the medical provider. It does not give you any say in the health care to be provided. So if your son or daughter balks at a painful or unpleasant procedure that you are certain would be beneficial, it will be his or her wishes that prevail—not yours.
- Your son or daughter can revoke the authorization at any time. No reason needs to be given. If a difficult situation arises, your son or daughter could withdraw consent, shutting you out altogether.

These scenarios would not occur if you were the legal guardian. In matters of medical care, the guardian's wishes always prevail, not those of the person under guardianship. As the legal guardian, you would have the right to learn the contents of all confidential communications between your son or daughter and the healthcare provider, no matter how personal.

If you ask your son or daughter to sign a medical Release form, make sure it is up to date with the HIPPA law (Health Insurance Portability and Accountability Act of 1996). Under HIPPA, in the name of privacy, medical providers may not share a patient's medical information with third parties—even immediate family members—without the patient's consent. To be effective, the release must specifically mention HIPPA. The Release form must also give an expiration date. There is a sample medical release in the Appendix.

Health Care Proxy

If there is a medical emergency, a health care proxy can allow you to take over and direct your son's or daughter's medical care. A person who is appointed to make healthcare decisions is called the healthcare agent. As the agent, you can authorize any treatment that your son or daughter could agree to if he or she were healthy and capable of giving consent. You can admit him or her to a hospital, consent to surgery, and approve follow up care.

A health care proxy can be important when there is a medical crisis, because it can avoid an emergency guardianship. That kind of court action could be required if a physician or hospital, for liability reasons, balks at treating a patient who is deemed to be unable to give informed consent to medical care.

But what if your son or daughter is reasonably healthy, and you just want to be able to direct his or her routine medical care? In that case, a health care proxy might not be effective. Under Massachusetts law, a health care proxy is only supposed to come into effect if and when a person is disabled and cannot participate in treatment decisions. However, in my experience, this point is largely ignored by the medical community. Most healthcare professionals accept the document as an expression of the person's desire to share medical decision making with the agent.

A health care proxy has some limitations:

- If the patient and the healthcare agent give conflicting instructions, the patient's wishes must prevail, not the agent's. So if your son or daughter refuses a treatment that you are certain would help, the healthcare provider must adhere to your son's or daughter's wishes, not yours.
- A health care proxy can be revoked at any time. This makes the health care proxy a less than ideal tool for someone who is attempting to manage the care of a person with mental health issues. Your agency could be abruptly revoked when you most need it—when your son or daughter is sick and refusing treatment.

If you ask your son or daughter to sign a health care proxy, make sure it specifically mentions HIPPA (discussed in the heath care proxy section). You don't want to give the healthcare providers any reason to question your authority.

Durable Power of Attorney

A durable power of attorney (DPA) can be an effective alternative to guardianship and conservatorship. (Chapter 18, "Conservatorship," covers this topic.) A DPA allows a person to appoint an agent to help with personal and financial management. Unlike guardianship, the person does not forfeit control. He or she merely appoints another person to act in certain specified areas.

A DPA that a young person might sign would give the agent the ability to do the following:

- Negotiate and sign the person's Individual Education Plan (IEP) or Individual Service Plan (ISP)
- Apply for and manage adult services from the various state agencies
- Appeal denials of benefits
- Hire attorneys, evaluators, and consultants to assist the person
- Sign income tax returns and other IRS forms
- Receive the person's mail or have the person's mail forwarded to the agent
- Apply for housing benefits
- Sign a lease for a house or apartment
- Order utility service
- Admit the person to a hospital, rehab facility, or nursing home
- Approve anti-psychotic medication, if that should be necessary
- Nominate a guardian or conservator if the person should become incapacitated and need a guardian or conservator

A DPA can be beneficial if a person becomes seriously ill or incapacitated. The DPA will continue to operate and be legally valid. This is the "durable" feature of the DPA.

There are some potential problems with DPAs. Third parties do not always recognize them. Some banks, insurance companies, and brokerage firms have their own power of attorney forms that they prefer their customers to use. To avoid any potential problems, ask the institutions you will be dealing with whether they will honor your

DPA. If they will not, you will have to obtain the necessary forms and ask your son or daughter to sign them.

Staleness can be another problem with a DPA. Although a DPA remains in effect indefinitely (or unless and until it is revoked), third parties (such as banks and other financial institutions) are sometimes reluctant to recognize a DPA that was signed several years earlier. If this occurs, you must obtain a certification stating that the DPA is still in effect and has not been revoked.

Another potential problem is that the DPA can be revoked at will. Your son or daughter can take away your authority at any time, without any prior notice. If this occurs, you must give written notice to all third parties with whom you transacted business. You must let them know that you are no longer authorized to act on the person's behalf.

13

Legal Requirements to Obtain Guardianship

Topics include

Limited guardianship
General guardianship
Will both parents be the legal guardians?
The public benefits dilemma

Let's say you have ruled out the alternatives to guardianship described in the previous chapter and have decided to proceed with the guardianship process. You should not expect the Court to appoint a guardian just because you ask it to do so. Instead, you must prove the legal elements of your case. This chapter describes the legal standards employed by the court.

An issue that can come up for some families is the choice of guardian. There are two public benefit programs that will pay a caregiver—including a parent—to provide care to a person with a disability. However, the programs will not pay the person's legal guardian. As a result, some parents face the difficult choice of either becoming the legal guardian or the paid caregiver. This chapter tells you what you need to know to make the decision.

Legal Standards

Before the court can appoint a guardian, there must be a hearing. Your son or daughter must attend the hearing unless there are compelling circumstances that excuse his or her presence. At the hearing, you must prove that your son or daughter needs a legal guardian and that you (or the person you select) are the best person to act in that role. You must present competent medical evidence pertaining to your son's or daughter's disability and attesting to the need for a guardian. The Court will only approve the guardianship if it is satisfied that your son or daughter:

- Has a significant, clinically diagnosed disability such as mental retardation, mental illness, or traumatic brain injury[10]
- Cannot adequately receive and evaluate information, or make or effectively communicate decisions
- Cannot meet essential requirements for physical health, safety, or self care
- Cannot be assisted to do any of the above with technology assistance

Limited and General Guardianship

How much decision-making authority do you want? Asked another way, how much authority do you think you can persuade the Court to give you? The answers to these questions will in part determine the kind of guardianship you apply for. You can ask to become the *limited guardian* or the *general guardian*. A guardian of a person who takes any so-called anti-psychotic medication is called a *Rogers* guardian (discussed in Chapter 15, "Special Situations."). If you want to manage your son's or daughter's finances, you must become a *conservator*. Chapter 18, "Conservatorship," covers this topic.

Limited guardianship

Under the new guardianship law that went into effect in July 2009, there is a preference for limited guardianship. The person with a disability is supposed to retain maximum independence. The courts are reluctant to take away a person's ability to make important decisions that affect his or her life.

---

10   Although most doctors and healthcare providers have replaced the term "mental retardation" with "intellectual disability," the Massachusetts courts still use the term "mental retardation." Therefore, this book will use the term "mental retardation" when it refers to the court process.

Let's say that your son or daughter has a rather complicated medical profile and needs you to oversee medical care. But let's also say that he or she is somewhat capable in other areas and has firm opinions about school, work, and friends. With a good deal of support, explanation, and supervision—which you will provide—he or she could reasonably understand the choices to be made and arrive at a sound decision. In that case, you could be the medical guardian, and your son or daughter would retain the ability to make all other decisions. This means that he or she could sign his or her Individual Education Plan (IEP) or Individual Support Plan (ISP), apply for services from the agencies that serve adults with disabilities, and sign contracts like leases, credit card agreements, and utility contracts.

General guardianship

In order to appoint a general guardian, the court must be satisfied that the person cannot reliably make any important decisions on his or her own. Limited guardianship must be ruled out as a possibility. Full guardianship may be appropriate if the person lacks the ability to process basic information or has very poor reasoning skills. A general guardian makes all major decisions for the person in areas such as medical care, living arrangements, work, and contracts. A general guardian can do things such as:

- Give consent to medical care
- Receive communications from medical providers
- Review the person's medical records
- Apply for and manage medical insurance and benefits, from both private insurers and public programs like MassHealth and Medicare
- Negotiate and sign the person's Individual Education Plan (IEP) or Individual Support Plan (ISP)
- Apply for and obtain services from the government agencies that serve adults with disabilities such as the state Department of Developmental Services, state Department of Mental Health, and Massachusetts Rehabilitation Commission
- Decide where the person will live

- Give consent (or refuse to consent) for vacations, day trips, etc.
- Give permission for a photograph of the person to be taken and shown for publicity purposes

Will Both Parents be the Guardians? The Public Benefits Dilemma

When parents have decided to seek guardianship, they usually expect to be co-guardians. This makes sense because they have both raised the child and know his or her needs best. If one parent dies after the guardianship has been put in place, the other parent can continue as the sole guardian.

But there can be a complicating factor if the family wants to participate in one of the MassHealth programs that will pay a caregiver—including the parent—of a person with a disability. There are currently two such programs:

- The Adult Family Care program will pay a caregiver to provide services in the caregiver's home.
- The Personal Care Attendant (PCA) Program will pay a caregiver to assist a person with a disability who lives in his or her own home.

There is detailed information about both programs, including the rates of compensation, in Chapter 10, "SSDI, Medicare, MassHealth, and Related Programs."

The complicating factor is that neither program will pay a person's legal guardian. If one parent (usually the mother) plans to be the paid caregiver, she cannot also be the legal guardian. Thus, in some families, the father will be the sole legal guardian so that the mother can be the paid caregiver. In other families, the father and an adult child—usually the one who will take over guardianship when both parents are gone—will be co-guardians.

The decision to exclude one parent from the guardianship role is a significant one. It is true that if the caregiver arrangement does not work out, you can return to court to change the guardianship orders.

But this can be time consuming and expensive. Thus, before you commit, you should be reasonably certain that having only one parent be the guardian will make sense on a long term basis. Consider the following factors:

- The amount of compensation the caregiver will receive. Will the funds provided for caregiving make it worthwhile? Also consider the amount of unpaid time you will need to spend doing things like filling out paperwork and meeting with agency personnel. The agency that manages the program for your area can tell you the details. The contact information is located in the Appendix.
- Convenience. The non-guardian parent may not be able to do things like sign routine paperwork and look at records. However, the inconvenience can be minimized by having the guardian sign an authorization (see below).
- Emotional factors. Being excluded from the guardian role may not feel right. If you are providing hands-on care and making day-to-day decisions, you probably want the rest of the world— doctors, school personnel, service providers, etc.—to recognize your authority.
- Longevity. Consider how long you plan to participate in the program. If your son or daughter will enter a residential situation in a year or two, a sole guardianship arrangement probably does not make sense. Also consider the possibility that the program rules may change favorably and allow a parent/guardian to participate. Conversely, also consider that the program funding may be reduced or eliminated.

Minimizing the inconvenience

The caregiver parent may need to do things such as take the son or daughter to the doctor, coordinate medical care among different providers, pick up medical records, sign routine forms, etc. But due to privacy laws, others may question the parent's authority to act. And what if a medical emergency should occur? The caregiver might not be able to authorize care.

A practical solution can be to have the guardian sign an authorization that gives the caregiver the authority to act on behalf of the child. The authorization can permit the caregiver to do anything the guardian could do if he or she were present—approve routine medical procedures as well as emergency care, obtain medical records, sign the IEP, and so forth. A sample Authorization is included in the Appendix.

14

The Court Process

Topics include

Finding an attorney
Medical Certificate
Clinical team report
The court hearing

This chapter explains the court process, including the paperwork and medical documents you will need to obtain guardianship. I also explain what happens at the court hearing. Hiring an attorney is also covered.

Getting Legal Help

Should you hire a lawyer or do the legal work yourself? The answer to this question will depend on several factors, including the cost of hiring counsel, your ability to pay, the complexity of the issues, your personal background and skills, the amount of time you have available, and your comfort level handling the matter yourself.

Before you hire a private attorney, find out whether the agency responsible for serving your son or daughter will handle the legal work for free. Sometimes the legal offices of the Massachusetts Commission for the Blind, Department of Mental Health, and Department of Developmental Services will represent parents who want to become the guardians.

Getting free legal help from one of these agencies is particularly useful if your son or daughter takes any antipsychotic medications (discussed in Chapter 15, "Special Situations"). The *Rogers* proceedings are quite complicated, especially in the first year when the medication treatment plan is initially put into place. Then the treatment plan must be reviewed periodically in court. It can be a relief to have a public agency take over the paperwork for this daunting and time-consuming task.

Court Forms

There are three basic forms that you will need to begin the guardianship: petition, bond, and either a clinical team report or a Medical Certificate (but not both). The guardianship forms can be obtained from any probate court or online at http://www.mass.gov/courts. All the forms are discussed separately in this section.

Petition

To begin a guardianship proceeding, use the form titled Petition for Appointment of Guardian of Adult Pursuant to M.G.L. c. 190B §5-303. Do not use the Guardian of a Minor form, even though your son or daughter may be under age 18. If you do, your guardianship authority will expire when your son or daughter reaches age 18, and you will need to begin the process again. You can fill in the form online and print it, or you can print the form and fill it in by hand.

The guardianship petition contains all the pertinent information about the proceeding. You can apply to be either the general guardian or the limited guardian. If you want to be the general guardian, you must specify why limited guardianship is not sufficient. If your son or daughter takes any antipsychotic medication, you must check the applicable boxes. This will prompt the Court to appoint an attorney for your son or daughter.

Bond

You must file a bond and have it approved by the Court. A bond is a pledge that you will faithfully perform your duties as the guardian and will not misuse your authority.

The bond can be either "with sureties" or "without sureties." A surety is an individual or insurance company who will act as your guarantor. If you cause any injury or financial loss to the person under guardianship and cannot compensate him or her, the surety could be required the pay the person out of his or her own funds.

In most cases, when a family member is the guardian, the bond can be without sureties.

Clinical team report

If the basis for the guardianship is an intellectual disability (which the court refers to as mental retardation) you will need a clinical team report. (You do *not* need a Medical Certificate.) The clinical team report must be completed by a registered physician, a licensed psychologist, and a licensed social worker. All three clinicians must have experience evaluating people with intellectual disabilities. Each one must evaluate the person before completing the report.

There are two different ways to obtain the clinical team report:

- You can locate three clinicians and have each of them meet separately with your son or daughter. One of the clinicians usually completes the report, and the other two clinicians sign the report, endorsing his or her findings. Alternatively, the clinicians who do not fill in the report can write a separate letter and attach it to the clinical team report. In most cases, the person's primary care doctor completes the medical piece. The school department may have a licensed psychologist and/ or social worker on the staff who can provide the other pieces. If not, your school department can probably refer you to a licensed person.
- You can have a guardianship evaluation performed by an agency or clinic that provides this service. The agency will arrange for all three parts of the evaluation. Before making the appointment, be sure to inquire if the provider will accept your health insurance.

Timing is important for the clinical team report. The guardianship petition must be filed with the court within 180 days after the evaluations have taken place. Otherwise, the Court may not accept the clinical team report, and you will have to obtain a new report.

Medical Certificate

If the basis for the guardianship is any disability other than intellectual disability, you must file a Medical Certificate. The Medical Certificate can be signed by a physician, licensed psychologist, or certified psychiatric nurse clinical specialist. The clinician must have personally examined your son or daughter.

Timing is important for the Medical Certificate. It is only valid for 30 days after the examination. Thus, you will need *two* Medical Certificates. The first one must be filed with the petition when you start the guardianship proceeding. Since that Medical Certificate will expire after 30 days, you will need another one for the court hearing. The second Medical Certificate must be dated, and the examination must have taken place, within 30 days prior to the court hearing. If the certificate has expired, the Court cannot approve the guardianship, and you will have to obtain a new Medical Certificate.

Filing the Paperwork

The forms needed to begin the guardianship process are the petition and clinical team report or Medical Certificate. The paperwork must be filed with the probate court for the county in which your son or daughter resides. However, if your son or daughter is in a hospital at the time you file, you must file in the county where the hospital is located. There are no filing fees.

When to file

You don't need to wait until your son or daughter reaches age 18 to apply for guardianship. The court can appoint a guardian before the 18th birthday. To be assured that your appointment will begin on or around your son's or daughter's birthday, plan to file the paperwork about ten to twelve weeks before the birthday.

Appointment of an attorney

If you request any special powers such as authority for antipsychotic medication, the Court will appoint an attorney to represent your son or daughter. The Court will also appoint an attorney if your son or daughter opposes any aspect of the guardianship.

Legal Notice

After the petition is filed, the Court will issue a legal notice (also called a citation). The purpose of the notice is to assure the Court that everyone who is legally entitled to have a say about your request to become the guardian has received notice and has been given an opportunity to be heard. The legal notice will contain instructions regarding the individuals and agencies that must be notified, as well as the method of notice. Be sure to carefully read the instructions in the legal notice.

Who must be notified

The legal notice must be given to your son or daughter and to all persons listed in the petition. If your son or daughter receives services from the Department of Developmental Services (formerly called the Department of Mental Retardation), that agency must be notified as well.

The legal notice will also specify a *return day*. That is the last day that anyone who has received a notice can object to the guardianship. The notices must be given within a certain period of time—usually seven to fourteen days—before the return day. Note that the return day is not the hearing date. The hearing must be scheduled with the Court.

Method of notice

The legal notice will contain instructions regarding the method of notice, such as by delivery, registered mail, certified mail, or publication in a newspaper. The legal notice and a copy of the petition must be handed to your son or daughter. This is true even though he or she would not understand their contents. A constable can give the papers to your son or daughter. Expect to pay about $35 to $50 for this service. An alternative is to have a "disinterested person" give the papers to your son or daughter. A disinterested person is someone who is not a party to the guardianship or related by blood to your son or daughter. Most people ask a family friend or sympathetic neighbor to assist them.

The petition and legal notice can be mailed to the other parties. A "certificate of mailing" should be obtained from the post office. Alternatively, a party can sign an Assent form (available from the probate court) indicating that he or she has received notice of the guardianship, consents to the guardianship, and agrees to your appointment as the legal guardian.

Return of service

After the required service (delivery and mailing) has been made, you or your attorney must sign the return of service on the second page of the citation, certifying that you have made service according to the court's order. Then the completed citation is filed with the court. If, after receiving the notice, your son or daughter opposes any aspect of the guardianship, you must tell the Court. An attorney will be appointed to represent your son's or daughter's interests. This is required by the new guardianship law.

The Hearing

Each probate court has its own procedures for guardianship hearings. And within each probate court, the individual judges have their own ways of doing things. The court staff or the judge's clerk will usually answer any questions you may have about what to expect.

Scheduling a hearing

In most courts, the court staff will let you choose the hearing date, subject to the judge's schedule. If an attorney has been appointed to represent your son or daughter, that person should be contacted to ensure that he or she will be available on the date you select.

Preparing for the hearing

Your son or daughter and the other parties must be notified of the hearing date. If counsel has been appointed, he or she must be notified as well.

On the hearing date, a Medical Certificate that is dated within 30 days of the hearing date must be on file along with a bond (if that form was not filed earlier). If you are seeking authority for antipsychotic medications, a Physician's Affidavit and Proposed Treatment Plan must also be filed. You must also prepare proposed Findings of Fact and a Treatment Plan for the judge to sign. If you are doing the legal work yourself, the judge's clerk might be willing to provide you with a sample form. Otherwise, you must have an attorney prepare those documents.

Your son or daughter must attend the hearing unless there are valid reasons to excuse his or her presence. If you do not want your son or daughter to come to court, the clinical team report or Medical Certificate should support your preferences.

What takes place at the hearing

The court hearing is a formal proceeding. The witnesses are sworn, and the proceedings are tape-recorded. You (or your attorney) may be asked to make a brief presentation to the Court, explaining why you are seeking guardianship and summarizing the contents of the medical evidence. If your son or daughter has counsel, the attorney will explain what he or she has done to investigate and also state whether he or she accepts or opposes the guardianship. The judge may also ask questions of counsel and the parties.

If any antipsychotic medication is involved, the hearing is usually longer and more involved. The judge must review the Physician's Affidavit and determine whether the proposed treatment with antipsychotic medications is in your son's or daughter's interest. The factors the Court must consider include your son's or daughter's expressed preferences; whether the proposed treatment would be contrary to your son's or daughter's religious beliefs; the benefits, risks, and possible side effects of the proposed medication; the prognosis (anticipated outcome) with treatment; and the prognosis without treatment.

After hearing the evidence, the judge will either approve or deny the guardianship. Alternatively, the judge could tailor the decree, giving you less authority than you have requested. For example, you could be granted authority to make only medical decisions instead of broad powers to make all personal decisions. If antipsychotic medications are involved, the judge will sign the Treatment Plan you provide and appoint a *Rogers* monitor.

The Decree

If the guardianship is approved, the judge will sign a guardianship decree that appoints one or more guardians. The decree is permanent and will remain in place unless and until the court revokes it. Upon request, the court staff will prepare a letter of appointment. You can get a certified copy of the letter of appointment—one that has a raised seal—from the copy department. There is no charge.

As noted above, when antipsychotic medications are involved, there will be a Treatment Plan, and a *Rogers* monitor will be appointed. The Treatment Plan and the monitor's authority are usually valid for one year. The Treatment Plan must be periodically renewed as long as your son or daughter takes any antipsychotic medications. The *Rogers* process is explained in detail in the next chapter.

15

Special Situations

Topics include

Antipsychotic medications
The *Rogers* process
Extraordinary medical procedures
Emergency guardianship

As noted in the previous chapter, a guardian does not have unlimited authority. There are some situations where the guardian must obtain prior court approval before acting. These include decisions about antipsychotic medications and extraordinary medical procedures. This chapter explains these special situations.

Antipsychotic Medications

For your son's or daughter's protection, special court proceedings are required if he or she takes any so-called antipsychotic (psychotropic) medications. These powerful drugs can sometimes cause severe side effects and even irreversible physical harm.

If your son or daughter takes one or more of these medications, then you, as the legal guardian, are not supposed to give them to him or her without a court order. Furthermore, you are not supposed to let another person, such as the school nurse or staff member at your son's or daughter's group home, administer them without court approval.

What are the antipsychotic medications?

Some examples of antipsychotic medications are Haldol, Risperdal, and Seroquel. Below, there is a list of all medications that are currently considered to be antipsychotics. This list may be updated as new drugs come on the market. To find out whether you will need court approval for any particular medication, you can ask the prescribing physician or look in the most recent edition of the *Physician's Desk Reference*. That publication is available at most public libraries. The Appendix contains a list of common medications (including antipsychotics) that are used to treat people with mental illness.

Antipsychotic medications

Trade name	Generic Name
Abilify	Aripiprazole
Clozaril	Clozapine
Geodon	Ziprasidone
Haldol	Haloperidol
Loxitane	Loxapine
Mellaril	Thioridazine
Moban	Molindone
Navane	Thiothixene
Orap	Pimozide
Prolixin	Fluphenazine
Risperdal	Risperidone
Serentil	Mesorizadine
Seroquel	Quetiapine fumate
Stelazine	Trifluoperazine
Thorazine	Chlorpromazine
Trilafon	Perphenazine
Zyprexa	Olanzapine

The *Rogers* Process

Before any antipsychotic medications can be given, a *Rogers* hearing must take place. *Rogers* proceedings are named after a 1983 Massachusetts court case, *Rogers v. Commissioner of Mental Health*.

That was the first case in which the Supreme Judicial Court ruled that antipsychotic medications are so intrusive and their side effects are so potentially severe, that only a Court—not a guardian—can authorize them.

At the *Rogers* hearing, the judge will review and either approve or deny a medication treatment plan. If the judge approves the plan, a *Rogers* monitor will be appointed. The *Rogers* monitor is usually, but not always, the same person as the guardian. The *Rogers* monitor's role is to keep close watch on the situation to make sure that the treatment plan is complied with and is effective. Treatment plans are temporary. Usually they expire after one year and must be brought back to court for annual reviews.

To initiate a *Rogers* proceeding, you must check off the boxes on the Guardianship Petition that state you want court authority for antipsychotic medications. The Court will appoint an attorney to represent your son or daughter. In most cases, the attorney's bill will be paid from public funds, unless your son or daughter has a substantial amount of personal assets.

As the petitioner, it is your responsibility to obtain a Physician's Affidavit from the psychiatrist who prescribes the medication. The Affidavit must state which antipsychotic medications are being proposed, the method of administration (oral, injection, etc.), and the dosage. The Affidavit plan must also describe the risks, benefits, and side effects of the proposed medications. It is common for the Affidavit to give a range of proposed dosages and to recommend alternative medications if the first choice is not effective or there are any side effects.

A hearing is required. At the hearing, you or your attorney must present the Affidavit and a proposed Treatment Plan to the Court. Your son's or daughter's attorney must attend the hearing to either consent to or oppose the Treatment Plan. At the hearing, the judge must be persuaded that the proposed medications are in your son's or daughter's best interest and that the risks do not outweigh the benefits.

In making a decision, the judge uses a process known as "substituted judgment." This means that the judge must determine whether the person would voluntarily choose to take the medication if he or she could think clearly about the situation and could express a preference. Since the psychiatric medications are supposed to help the person get better, and presumably most people, if given a choice, would want to get better, most judges usually decide in favor of the medications. However, each person is unique, and different circumstances require different results.

If the judge approves the treatment plan, he or she will appoint the guardian (or another person) to be the *Rogers* monitor. As mentioned above, the treatment plan usually expires after one year and must be reviewed annually as long as the person needs such medications. If your son or daughter receives services from the Department of Developmental Services or the Department of Mental Health, you can ask the agency's legal department to take over the annual reviews. Their services are free of charge.

Role of the *Rogers* monitor

As the *Rogers* monitor, your role is to make sure that:

- Your son or daughter receives only the antipsychotic drugs listed on the treatment plan
- The dosages do not exceed the maximum listed on the treatment plan
- Your son or daughter does not experience any adverse side effects

To do your job, you must familiarize yourself with the treatment plan and also attend any medication reviews. These reviews usually take place at the treating psychiatrist's office at least quarterly, and in some cases, monthly. To monitor the medication's effects, including any side effects, you can rely on personal observations as well as reports from staff and others who work with your son or daughter. If you think that the medication is not helping and may even be harmful, you should discuss your concerns with the physician right away.

What if you learn that the treatment plan is not being followed? In that case, you should notify both the medical staff at your son's or daughter's program or residence as well as the prescribing psychiatrist. If the situation is not promptly remedied, you can contact the attorney who was assigned to represent your son or daughter in the *Rogers* proceeding. If necessary, the matter can be brought forward in court for an emergency hearing.

Extraordinary Medical Treatments

Other medical decisions that require a guardian to obtain prior court approval include:

- Electro-convulsive treatments (ECT or "shock" treatments)
- Psychosurgery
- Abortion
- Any surgery that would cause a person to become sterile (even if the purpose of the procedure is to alleviate an underlying medical condition)
- Withdrawal of potentially life-saving treatments, such as artificial hydration, artificial nutrition, or life support

If your son or daughter needs any of the above treatments, the healthcare provider will require the guardian to obtain a court order. The Court will appoint an attorney to represent the interests of the person with a disability. A "substituted judgment" hearing must take place, at which the judge determines what kind of care the person would choose if he or she were competent and able to decide. There must be specific written findings that include, among other things, why the benefits of the proposed procedure outweigh the drawbacks.

Emergency Guardianship

If there is a medical emergency and you need guardianship right away, you can ask the court to appoint a temporary guardian. The person the court appoints will have authority to act for up to 90 days. In order for the Court to grant the request, either a Medical Certificate or a clinical team report (whichever one applies to the person's situation) must be filed. The Medical Certificate can usually be promptly completed by the physician who is recommending the medical procedure. However, the clinical team report is more problematic. All three clinicians (the physician, licensed psychologist, and licensed social worker) must each personally evaluate the person before completing the report. This can make the process rather prolonged. All this illustrates why it is best to plan in advance by having the guardianship in place on or shortly before your son's or daughter's 18th birthday.

16

The Guardian's Responsibilities

Topics include

Reporting to the Court
Human rights and dignity
Giving informed consent
Record keeping
Guardianship fees

Now that the Court has made you the legal guardian, you may be wondering what you need to do. Guardians have responsibilities that are not described in the guardianship decree or in the court rules. This chapter explains those responsibilities. Guardianship fees are also covered. Since guardians sometimes have questions about their own personal liability, this chapter also explains steps you can take to protect yourself from financial loss.

Reporting to the Court

The Uniform Probate Code that took effect July 1, 2009, contains new reporting requirements for guardians.

All guardians who are appointed on or after July 1, 2009, must file:

- A Care Plan. The Care Plan describes the guardian's plans for the person's future care and explains how the guardian plans to improve the person's ability to make decisions. The Care Plan must be filed within 60 days of the appointment.

- An Annual Report. The Annual Report includes, among other things, the person's overall status, living arrangements, and the guardian's contacts with him or her. The guardian must account for any funds under his or her control, such as SSI or SSDI for which the guardian is the representative payee. The guardianship decree will state when the Annual Report is due.

All guardians who were appointed before July 1, 2009, must file Annual Reports (see above). The first report would be due on the first anniversary date of the appointment after July 1, 2009.

> The court appointed John's mother to be his guardian on November 21, 2002. The first annual report would be due on November 21, 2010.

The Care Plan and Annual Reports must be filed with the Court and given to the person under guardianship and to all other persons listed on the Petition. This would include both parents and siblings of the person under guardianship.

The Care Plan/Report form can be obtained from any probate court or online at http://www.mass.gov/courts.

Protection

A guardian's duty is to protect the person under guardianship, to advocate for him or her, and to put his or her needs above the guardian's needs in all matters relating to the guardianship.

Basic needs

Protecting the person means making sure that his or her basic needs are met. The person must have a safe place to live, adequate food and clothing, and access to medical care.

Human rights and dignity

Protecting the person's human rights and dignity is also important.

Human rights are the fundamental respect that we owe one another as individuals, regardless or our comparative abilities.

To protect the civil and human rights of its clients, the Department of Developmental Services (DDS) has enacted its own "Standards to Promote Dignity." These standards cover areas such as privacy, communication, medication, and behavior plans. The DDS standards are published in the Code of Massachusetts Regulations at 115 CMR 5.00-5.16. They can be found online at http://www.lawlib.state.ma.us.

Similar protections are afforded to clients of the Department of Mental Health. The Department's standards to promote dignity are located at 104 CMR 28.00-28.12.

In addition, as a licensing requirement, all DDS and DMH service providers must develop written procedures to protect their clients' human rights. Each provider must also designate a human rights officer to address any problems. The protections commonly ensure the clients' rights to:

- Receive equal protection under the law, such as the right to be free from discrimination based on one's race, gender, age, religion, disability, or sexual orientation
- Make meaningful choices about their lives, such as where and with whom to live, what to eat, and with whom to communicate
- Have personal friendships and intimate relationships with other consenting adults
- Have privacy in their personal spaces and the right to confidentiality
- Keep and use their own personal possessions

What should you do if you think your son's or daughter's human rights may have been violated? Immediately bring this to the attention of the agency that serves your son or daughter. Alternatively, you can tell your son's or daughter's case manager. (The case manager is the person assigned by a state agency, such as DDS or DMH, to oversee your son's or daughter's care.) The case manager must investigate your concerns.

Another option is to complain directly to the Disabled Persons Protection Commission by calling 1-800-426-9009. The hotline is staffed 24 hours a day, seven days a week. The DPPC is empowered to investigate reports of suspected human rights violations as well as reports of abuse or neglect and to recommend sanctions against wrongdoers.

Advocacy

A guardian also has a responsibility to make sure that the person is receiving all potential public benefits. These benefits could include case management, a day program, transportation, a housing subsidy, and residential services. Perhaps the person may be entitled to services from more than one agency. In that case, you might need to seek funding from the Department of Developmental Services, Department of Mental Health, Department of Public Health, or Massachusetts Commission for the Blind. To secure the services, you might need to hire an advocate or a benefits manager. Any fees incurred can be paid from the person's funds.

Giving Informed Consent

Guardians are sometimes asked to approve medical procedures and medications. These can range from the routine (annual exam, flu shot, or basic dental care) to the complex (colonoscopy, major surgery requiring anesthesia, or even an organ transplant). Some of the medical procedures you may be asked to approve could involve serious risks to the person, and the medications could cause significant side effects.

How do you go about making the decision? Giving informed consent means making a decision based on all the pertinent available information. To make a sound decision, you must consider, among other things, the nature of the treatment or procedure being proposed, its purpose, risks, benefits, and alternatives.

Obtaining information

How do you obtain the necessary information? Certainly you will need to talk to the doctors involved, both the one recommending the procedure and the one performing it (if they are different). Make an appointment to meet in person or talk on the telephone. But before your conference, do some background research to know what questions to ask. To do this, I usually visit one or more of the informative medical-based web sites located on the Internet, such as Medline (Medlineplus. gov) or Medscape (Medscape.com).

Questions to ask

After you have done your research, formulate the questions you want to ask and write them down. At a minimum, you should inquire:

- What is the person's condition that requires treatment?
- Is he or she currently being treated for the condition? If so, how?
- In what way is the current treatment not working?
- What treatment is now being recommended?
- What is the rationale for the treatment?
- What symptoms or conditions is the treatment supposed to address?
- How will we assess if the treatment is effective? (In other words, do we expect a 75 percent reduction in symptoms, 50 percent, or less?)
- What is the time frame for assessing whether the treatment is effective?
- Is the situation urgent or can the treatment safely be postponed?
- What is the prognosis (anticipated outcome) with treatment?
- What is the prognosis without treatment?
- What are the risks of the treatment?
- What are the benefits of the treatment?
- Should you obtain a second opinion?
- Does the treatment have any possible side effects? If so, what are they, and what is the likelihood they will occur?
- What is the "track record" of the procedure? How likely is it to be safe and effective?
- Will any follow-up care be needed? If so, are there staff or other caregivers who can assist the person to recover?
- Are there any alternatives to the proposed treatment? If so, what are they?

- Have the alternative treatments been considered? If not, why not?

Involving the person under guardianship

To what extent, if at all, should you involve your son or daughter in medical decision making? In general, that depends on his or her ability to understand and participate. Certainly if your son or daughter is able to grasp that he or she is ill and needs treatment, then the proposed procedures, including the risks and benefits, should be explained. But even if your son or daughter balks at an unpleasant procedure—or willingly agrees to an especially risky one—that does not necessarily mean that you must follow his or her wishes. Instead, your son's or daughter's expressed preference is but one of several factors you must use to make your decision.

Second opinions

Perhaps after speaking with the doctor, you still can't decide. If so, don't hesitate to consult another doctor. Most insurance companies will pay for a second surgical opinion.

Declining treatment

Perhaps after considering all the available information, you feel that the proposed treatment is not advisable. In that case, don't be afraid to decline the treatment. Disagreeing with the doctor is your prerogative as the medical guardian. After all, the right to consent to treatment also includes the right to say no.

Record Keeping

Most likely your guardianship activities will generate a lot of paperwork. A good record keeping system is essential to keeping things organized and under control. What records do guardians need to keep and for how long? Generally, anything that relates to the person's legal, medical, or financial situation should be retained. Although there are no hard and fast rules on how long records need to be kept, my own practice is to keep these kinds of records for at least ten years. If any income tax returns have been filed, most experts recommend that copies of the returns for at least six prior years should be retained. This will protect you if the Internal Revenue Service audits you.

For my own family and also for my clients, my guardianship files are quite comprehensive and include these kinds of information:

My *legal* files contain copies of the court paperwork, including a few extra photocopies of my guardianship appointment. I usually don't keep any extra certified copies of the court appointment, because in most cases the certification expires after six months.

The *medical* files hold copies of the annual physical and dental exams, insurance cards, medical reports, lab results, and annual consent forms, including any standing orders. If a doctor recommends a particular procedure, I keep notes of my conversations with the doctor regarding what is involved, why he or she thinks the procedure is necessary, the risks and benefits, and so forth. For any medications, I keep notes of the dosage, dates, and any observations about the medication's effectiveness or adverse side effects. If there is Medicare or private insurance, I usually keep the benefit statements for at least two years.

When I serve as the *Rogers* monitor for a client, I keep a separate file that includes the treatment plan and all reports of medication reviews. These reviews take place at least quarterly and sometimes monthly.

An *IEP* file holds the current Individual Education Plan and quarterly progress notes. My adult clients' files contain their Individual Service Plans and notes from the ISP meetings.

Guardianship Fees

A guardian has a right to charge a fee for his or her services. Most parents do not charge a fee. However, other relatives sometimes do, and the possibility of compensation might persuade a reluctant relative to take on the guardian role. Any fees can be paid from the person's funds, if there are any, or from the person's special needs trust.

There are no set fees that guardians charge. Professional guardians (such as attorneys, financial professionals, and social workers) sometimes charge their usual hourly rate. This is based on their qualifications and experience.

Guardians who are not professionals set their fee according to factors like the amount of funds available, the time involved, and the complexity of the duties. A guardian would probably charge a lower rate for paying bills or traveling to appointments (perhaps $15 to $20 per hour) than for meeting with doctors or lawyers or attending court hearings (perhaps $50 to $75 per hour). Some guardians charge an hourly rate for time actually spent, while others charge the same flat rate every month.

Protecting Yourself

What if a person under guardianship runs up bills he or she cannot pay, or hurts someone, or damages someone's property? Must the guardian pay out of his or her own funds? No. Just because you are your son's or daughter's legal guardian does not make you personally responsible for his or her actions. Damaged property and unpaid bills are the person's financial responsibility, not yours. But if you are the conservator, you must use the funds under your control to make restitution.

What if a person under guardianship needs a contract signed, such as a loan agreement or an apartment lease? When signing these kinds of legal documents, there are steps you can take to protect yourself. You should make it clear that you are acting only as the person's legal guardian and not on your own behalf. To do so, under the signature line, print the person's name, your own name, and your capacity (for example, "John Smith, by his legal guardian Mary Smith"). Then, when you sign the document, write "John Smith, by Mary Smith, his legal guardian" or words to that effect. That way, it is clear that you are acting only in a fiduciary capacity and that you are not pledging your personal credit if the person cannot pay.

17

Financial Management

Topics include

Single transactions through the probate court
Representative payment for government benefits
Durable Power of Attorney
Special Needs Trust

If your son or daughter needs help to manage his or her finances, you could apply to the probate court to become the conservator. A conservator manages the income and assets of a person with a disability.[11]

I usually advise parents not to become their son's or daughter's conservator if there is a reasonable alterative for managing finances. All conservators must comply with a rigorous court-ordered accounting process that requires filing annual accounts with the Court explaining how the person's money has been invested and spent. Depending on the amount of money involved, there may be a filing fee for the accounts. The Court will usually appoint a guardian *ad litem* (GAL) to review the accounts on the person's behalf. The GAL fees, which are paid from the person's funds, can be steep.

Most families would prefer not to burden themselves with a time-consuming and expensive court process if they do not have to. Fortunately, there are several easy ways to manage the finances of a

---

11 Under the law in effect before July 1, 2009, someone who managed the finances of a person with a disability through the court was called the "guardian of the estate." That term has been eliminated under the new law. However, although the terminology is different, guardians of the estate who were appointed before July 1, 2009, can continue to manage the person's finances.

person with a disability that do not require court involvement. These alternatives to conservatorship are the subject of this chapter.

Single Transactions Authorized by the Probate Court

When a person with a disability inherits money or receives compensation for an injury, the funds are often transferred to a special needs trust. This can assure that the person's public benefits will not be disrupted and that the funds will be properly managed. You can ask the probate court to approve the transfer. When the transfer is complete, you will not have any further responsibilities to the court.

Representative Payment for Government Benefits

If a person who receives any government benefits such as SSI or SSDI needs help to manage them, the Social Security Administration will appoint a person to receive the benefits on the person's behalf. This is called a *representative payee*, or *rep payee*, arrangement. The check can be deposited directly into a special bank account the rep payee maintains for the benefits. The funds can be used to purchase items and services the recipient needs. Chapter 5, "Representative Payment," discusses these arrangements.

Joint Bank Account

An easy way to assist a person with a disability to manage a small amount of money is a joint bank account. The person might learn to write checks, make purchases, and even balance the account. To minimize the risk of loss, do not keep any more money in the account than you can afford to lose.

Be advised, however, that a joint bank account is not appropriate if you are the rep payee for government benefits such as SSI and SSDI. Under the Social Security rules, only the rep payee—not the recipient— is supposed to have access to the rep payee bank account.

Durable Power of Attorney

In Chapter 12, "Alternatives to Guardianship," I explained how a Durable Power of Attorney can sometimes be an effective alternative to guardianship. A person who has legal capacity can appoint an agent to do things like coordinate medical care, negotiate and sign the IEP or ISP, and appeal decisions denying adult services.

A Durable Power of Attorney can also help a person with a disability avoid conservatorship by delegating financial management to an agent. Unlike conservatorship, the person does not lose control of his or her finances. He or she merely appoints the agent to assist in certain specified areas. Some typical financial powers that a young person might delegate to an agent include:

- Endorse and deposit checks payable to the person
- Open a bank account
- Sign checks to pay bills
- Use an investment account to manage assets
- Buy or sell property, including real estate
- Use the person's money to make gifts
- Establish a trust for the person's benefit and transfer his or her funds to the trust

Special Needs Trust

If a person with a disability receives an inheritance or injury award, a special needs trust can be a useful way to manage the funds.

A special needs trust generally provides two kinds of benefits for a person with a disability:

- A trustee can manage the funds under a formal written arrangement. The trustee has a fiduciary responsibility to assure that the funds are properly invested, earn a reasonable rate of return, and are used solely for the beneficiary's personal needs. The trustee must periodically account to the beneficiary (or his or her legal representative) for the funds under the trustee's control.

- A special needs trust can allow a person with a disability to qualify for most government benefit programs. This is true even if those programs require, as a condition of eligibility, that a person can only have limited income and resources. Most such "need based" programs do not include a special needs trust within the definition of resources.

The funds held in a special needs trust may be used to purchase items and services that government benefits do not provide. These include recreation, vacations, travel, special therapies, paid staff or companions, and personal items such as furniture, a computer, software, music player, and sports equipment.

The special needs trust must be irrevocable. This means that once the trust has been established and the funds have been transferred to the trustee, the person cannot change his or her mind and get the money back.

Another important point is that only the trustee, not the beneficiary, can control how the funds will be used.

Chapter 3, "Reducing Assets to Qualify for SSI," discusses special needs trusts in detail. Chapter 28, "Money Matters," discusses the pros and cons of saving money through a special needs trust.

18

Conservatorship

Topics include

Conservatorship basics
Reporting to the Court
The conservator's responsibilities

The alternatives to conservatorship described in the previous chapter may not be appropriate because of a person's level of functioning. And sometimes families feel more comfortable having the assets protected and supervised by the probate court. In either case, conservatorship may be appropriate.

Conservatorship Basics

You begin the court process for conservatorship by filing a Petition for Appointment of a Conservator and a bond with the court. You must also file a Medical Certificate or a clinical team report (whichever one applies to your situation). See Chapter 14, "The Court Process."

You can ask to be a *general* or a *limited* conservator. If there is a *general* conservator, the person's rights can be quite restricted. He or she will not be able to endorse paychecks, maintain a bank account, or control any of his or her own funds.

As the name suggests, a *limited* conservator only handles some of the person's funds. For example, a person under a limited conservatorship (called a "protected person") might retain all his earnings from employment. The conservator would manage the person's other assets like investments and real estate. In another example, a person might be able to keep a limited amount of funds (say, $5,000) in her own name, and the conservator would manage everything else.

The paperwork is filed in the probate court for the county in which your son or daughter resides.

The court will issue a legal notice (also called a citation) that must be given to your son or daughter and to all other persons listed on the petition. The process for giving legal notices is the same one used in guardianship proceedings. (See the Legal Notice section of Chapter 14, "The Court Process.").

After the return day, a hearing can take place. If the Court approves the conservatorship, it will issue a decree appointing the conservator. The court will also issue a letter of appointment that can be shown to third parties. The letter of appointment will allow the conservator to take charge of the person's assets and manage them for his or her benefit.

Reporting to the Court

A conservator has three basic reporting requirements:

- The Court can order the conservator to file a Financial Plan for managing, spending, and distributing the person's assets. (A conservator can ask the Court to waive this requirement.) The plan must be based on the person's actual needs and take into account his or her best interests. The plan must include any steps the conservator plans to take to assist the person to manage his or her own property, an estimate of how long the conservatorship will last, and a projection of the expenses the conservator will incur. The Conservator's Financial Plan and Guidelines for Preparing the Financial Plan are available on the probate court website (http://www.mass.gov/courts/courtsandjudges/courts/probateandfamilycourt/upcforms.html).
- Within 90 days of the appointment, a conservator must file a detailed inventory of the person's assets. A copy of the inventory form must be given to the person under conservatorship, even if he or she would not understand it. A Sample Conservator's

Inventory and Instructions for Preparing the Inventory are available on the probate court website.

- A conservator must file annual financial accounts with the court that show how the funds have been managed. The accounts must show the income, expenses, and how the funds are invested. Depending on the amount of money involved, there may be a filing fee for the accounts.[12] Periodically, the accounts must be approved by the Court. An attorney will be appointed to act as guardian ad litem (GAL) on behalf of the person under conservatorship. The GAL's fees are paid from the funds under management. A Conservator's Account, Simplified Accounting Guidelines for Estate and Conservator Accounts, and Sample Conservator's Account can be found on the probate court website.

In addition to these reporting requirements, the Court also requires a conservator to keep suitable records of the funds. The conservator must show the records to any person with a legal interest in the conservatorship who asks to see them.

Responsibilities to the Person under Conservatorship

A conservator has an obligation to put the protected person's interest above his or her own interest in all matters relating to the conservatorship.

Funds must benefit the person under conservatorship

The conservator has a duty to use the person's funds just for him or her alone. The funds should not benefit anyone else. The funds should not be given away. However, it is all right to use the person's money to buy modest gifts for friends and family on birthdays, holidays, or other special occasions.

---

12 Currently there is no fee if the amount under management is less than $10,000.

Self-dealing

A conservator should not borrow the person's money or loan the money to friends or relatives. This is true even if the terms are more favorable than the person could obtain from a commercial lender. These kinds of transactions between the conservator (or his friends and relatives) and the protected person are called self-dealing. Self-dealing is widely considered to be a violation of the conservator's duty of loyalty to the person.

Prudent investments

The protected person's funds should be invested to generate a reasonable rate of return. The money should not sit in a non-interest-bearing account. Still, the funds should be invested prudently and conservatively. The appropriate types of investments depend on, among other things, the amount of money to be invested and the person's age, health, and immediate and long-term needs.

For example, if the person is in relatively good health and his or her needs for housing and medical care are currently being met, the investments could emphasize long-term growth. But if the person is in poor health and has few other resources, the investments might be weighted more toward income-producing assets.

When it comes to investments, a knowledgeable financial adviser can be an invaluable asset. The adviser can help you identify investment goals and then recommend a specific strategy. Some advisers can even take over managing the investments. The adviser's fees can be paid from the person's funds.

In choosing a financial advisor, be sure to select one who is knowledgeable about people with disabilities and public benefits. (See the Resources section.)

19

Frequently Asked Questions about Guardianship

Topics include

Voting
Death or resignation of the guardian
Co-guardians

1. *Can a person under a general guardianship vote?*

Yes. Although there are laws on the books in Massachusetts that appear to bar people under guardianship from voting, these laws are not currently being enforced. In fact, people with disabilities are encouraged to vote. The Department of Developmental Services includes a person's desire to vote or not vote in all its client service plans. Most communities have trained their public employees to accommodate people who want to register. To sign up to vote, the person just needs to go to the Clerk's office in the city or town where he or she resides.

2. *Can a person under a general guardianship make a will?*

Yes. However, the person must be able to understand the basics of what he or she is signing and be free from coercion. This means that the person must know the nature and amount of property that he or she owns and understand that he or she is writing a will to dispose of that property upon his or her death. Also, for the will to be valid, no one can be forcing the person to write the will or pressuring the person to make an unnatural disposition of property. An example would be a caregiver pressuring a person to leave his property to the caregiver instead of to the person's relatives or close friends.

3. Is there a benefit to having co-guardians?

Sometimes having co-guardians can maximize the chances that someone will be available to act if the guardian is temporarily absent, such as on a ten-day ocean cruise.

Also, having co-guardians can sometimes avoid the necessity of court proceedings if one guardian cannot serve due to death, disability, or for some other reason. In some families, a parent and child will serve as co-guardians of a family member with a disability. When the parent dies, the child can continue to act. However, this arrangement would exclude one parent from decision making (assuming that both parents are living). Also, both guardians would have to agree on most major issues such as living arrangements, work, and medical care. That is not always possible in every family.

4. Is a guardian required to use his or her own funds to support the person?

No. Siblings are sometimes concerned that by agreeing to take on the role of guardian, they will also take on the financial responsibility of supporting their brother or sister with a disability. This is not the case. A guardian does not have to spend his or her own personal resources. A guardian only needs to use the person's own funds for his or her support.

5. To whom should the guardian give a copy of the appointment?

The regular healthcare providers (primary care doctor and dentist) should have a copy of the letter of appointment. If any medical procedures such as tests or operations are scheduled, the provider or hospital should also have a copy of the appointment. Your son's or daughter's school or adult service provider should be given a copy. In effect, notifying these individuals and entities that you are the legal guardian gives them notice that you—and not your son or daughter—must be consulted about any major issues that affect him or her.

6. *If the guardianship does not mention any antipsychotic medications, but the doctor prescribes them later, what can be done?*

The guardianship can be amended to give the guardian authority to consent to treatment with antipsychotic medications. You do not need to start from the beginning with a new petition and a new clinical team report or Medical Certificate. However, you will need an Affidavit as to Competency and Proposed Treatment Plan from a physician.

7. *What if the person's functioning improves to the point where the guardianship is no longer needed?*

Sometimes people with disabilities get better. This can occur for any number of reasons—a supportive, stable living environment, the right medication or combination of medications, acquired life skills, improved physical health and better cognitive functioning, or just age and maturity.

If the person's functioning improves to the point where the guardian has too much control, the guardian's powers can be made less restrictive. For example, perhaps there is a general guardianship, but now the person only needs help with medical decisions. In that case, the guardian's powers can be limited to the medical arena. If the person is able to make all decisions on his or her own, the guardianship can be vacated.

Part III: Estate Planning

THIS SECTION WILL EXPLAIN how to develop a sound estate plan to protect your family after you are gone.

I start by taking a look at what could happen if you don't do any planning. The possibilities might surprise you. Your child with a disability might lose important government benefits because of the way you left the heritance. Your children without disabilities might get their inheritances sooner than you would like. If there is a former spouse or partner in your past, he or she could end up with your children—and their money.

Perhaps you are now convinced that you need to do something. But what? For starters, don't disinherit your child with a disability or leave his or her inheritance to a sibling without disabilities to hold. You won't be doing your family any favors, and disappointment is sure to follow.

To do things properly, most people who have a child with a disability should have a will and a special needs trust. If you want to go beyond the basics, I explain how to use trusts for special situations, such as reducing estate taxes, avoiding probate, and protecting a child's inheritance from a former spouse or partner.

While you are planning for your child with a disability, don't overlook the possibility that you could become disabled yourself. I explore some strategies to maintain control of your healthcare decision-making and finances.

Another topic you need to consider is how much money your family would need if you were gone. You can create an instant estate by buying life insurance. However, you need to know how much insurance to buy. There are some guidelines to help you decide.

Saving money is another topic that comes up. Sometimes children receive savings bonds and other monetary gifts on birthdays, holidays, and other special occasions. What is the best way to save money until your child needs it? Should you save money through a special needs trust? There are some guidelines to help you decide.

Many people have questions about protecting their assets. After all, an estate plan may not do your family much good if you don't have any assets to pass along. I discuss some easy, low-cost strategies to protect your residence.

Let's start by looking at why you should plan and what could happen if you don't.

20

Why Plan?

Topics include

What could happen if you do not plan?
Do not disinherit your child with a disability
Use a special needs trust to protect a child with a disability

To appreciate the benefits of advance planning, it helps to understand what could happen if you don't plan. This chapter describes some possible scenarios. When it comes to your child with a disability, however, doing "something" isn't necessarily always better than doing nothing—especially if "something" involves disinheriting your child or asking a sibling to hold the inheritance. Instead, you should use a special needs trust to protect your child after you are gone.

What Could Happen if You Do Not Plan?

Here are some possibilities to consider.

Your son's or daughter's inheritance could be mismanaged or lost.

If your child with a disability cannot properly manage an inheritance, he or she could be financially exploited. Losing public benefits is also a concern. Most public entitlement programs require a person to be poor. A child with a disability who receives even a modest inheritance might not qualify for those programs. To protect your child with a disability after your death, use a special needs trust. Chapter 23, "Using a Special Needs Trust to Plan Your Estate," discusses these trusts.

Your son's or daughter's money could revert to the state.

If your son or daughter with a disability inherits any money from your estate, he or she might be able to preserve public benefits by putting the inherited funds in a special needs trust. However, when your son or daughter passes on, any remaining trust funds must be used to reimburse the state for his or her Medicaid benefits. Most parents prefer that any unspent trust funds pass to their children without disabilities or to other relatives, instead of the state. To benefit *all* your children, use a special needs trust. (See Chapter 23, "Using a Special Needs Trust to Plan Your Estate.")

Your children could become comfortably wealthy—at age 18.

In Massachusetts, a minor child (under age 18) who receives any property through an estate is entitled to receive the full inheritance at age 18 (21 at the latest). If you don't want this to happen, you must use proper planning to delay the distribution of your children's inheritances. The money can be held and managed by a person you select until your children reach a more mature age (such as 25 or 28).

Your least favorite relative might raise your children.

When both parents have died, the court will usually appoint a legal guardian—in most cases, a relative—to act as a surrogate parent until the children reach age eighteen. Sometimes the person the court picks to raise the children is not the person the parents would have chosen. You can make sure the people you trust will be in charge by using a will to nominate one or more guardians for your minor children. Chapter 22, "Using a Will to Plan Your Estate." explains this.

If you are a single or divorced parent, your former spouse or partner could raise your minor children and get control of their money.

If a single or divorced parent dies, the surviving parent is usually the one to raise the children and manage their inheritance. For some parents, this can be anxiety provoking, especially if there are substance abuse, gambling, or creditor issues. There may not be much you can do to prevent your former spouse or partner from raising your children. However, you can prevent him or her from getting control of your children's money by using a revocable trust. Chapter 26 "Beyond the Basics," discusses these trusts.

A stranger could manage your affairs.

Most of us would not want a stranger going through our personal effects after we are gone. Yet that might happen if the court picks someone you don't know to manage your estate. You can put a person you know and trust in charge by using a will to nominate an executor.

Assets could be diverted from your spouse to your children.

On death, any assets you own in your own name will pass to your legal heirs according to state law. In Massachusetts, this means that your spouse will only receive one-half of your separately owned property. The rest of the property will pass to your children, including children who are minors or who have disabilities. That could leave your surviving husband or wife without enough money to live comfortably.

As I explained earlier, if your child with a disability receives any assets directly in his or her own name, government assistance that is based on financial need could be lost. To prevent this, you can use a will or trust to make sure your assets go to your spouse, not your children.

The probate process can create costs and delays.

On death, a person's separately owned property must pass through probate. Probate is the court process by which your assets are inventoried, your debts are paid, and the remaining property is distributed according to your will, or to your legal heirs if you do not have a valid will. The probate process can be lengthy and expensive. But you can use a living trust to reduce or even eliminate probate costs and delays. Chapter 26, "Beyond the Basics," discusses living trusts.

Estate taxes could reduce the amount your survivors will receive.

Depending on the amount of assets you own at the time of your death, federal and Massachusetts estate taxes could be imposed on your estate.[13] Such taxes could significantly reduce the amount of money you can pass to your survivors. With proper planning, you can minimize or even eliminate estate taxes and leave more property to your heirs. Chapter 26, "Beyond the Basics," discusses federal and Massachusetts estate taxes.

Plans That Do Not Work

I hope that I have convinced you that planning is better than doing nothing. Still, when it comes to your children with disabilities, some strategies don't work. These tactics include disinheriting your son or daughter with a disability or giving your child's inheritance to your non-disabled child to hold. Although these strategies rarely work, some families use them. Here are three "plans" to avoid.

Do not disinherit your child with a disability

Some parents think they should disinherit their son or daughter with a disability, because then their child's needs will be taken care of by the state. They reason that it is preferable to leave their assets to their children without disabilities, who can use the assets to pay for higher education, purchase a home, or get started in a business. They think this is better than giving assets to their child with a disability, who will not need them or know how to use them.

There is some logic to this reasoning, because as a general rule, in order for the state to assume the financial cost of supporting a person with a disability, the person must have very few financial resources.

---

13 Under the current estate tax law, there is no federal estate tax beginning in January 2010. In 2011, federal estate taxes will be imposed on estates worth more than $1 million. However, most analysts expect Congress to change the law in 2010 so that only estates worth $3.5 million or more will be taxed. In Massachusetts, estate taxes are imposed on estates that have assets of more than $1 million that are passed to people other than the surviving spouse.

But what some parents do not understand (or choose to ignore) is that government benefits are uncertain. There is no guarantee they will always be adequately funded or even available. And even if government benefits are in place to provide basic support, they do not necessarily provide everything a person with a disability needs to have a good quality of life. If your son's or daughter's favorite activities include regular restaurant meals, an annual vacation, or trips to Fenway Park, wouldn't you want these pleasures to continue after you are gone? If so, disinheriting your son or daughter is not the answer.

Do not leave any money outright to your child with a disability

If a child's disability is relatively minor, some parents feel it is better to leave the money outright for him or her to enjoy. When the money runs out, they reason, he or she can always turn to public benefits for support. In other families, there is no one who can act as a trustee, so money is left directly to the person with a disability.

One of the problems with this approach is that you lose control. If a person cannot properly manage his or her funds or is being financially exploited, no one can help without the person's express permission. Even if the person eventually asks for help, it may be too late. Sometimes a person's legal options become limited with the passage of time.

Do not leave your child's money to a sibling

Another strategy that is sometimes recommended is to leave the child's inheritance to a sibling to hold. In that way, nothing is shown on paper that the person with a disability has inherited anything, whether outright or in trust. And by not inheriting, some parents assume, their son or daughter can retain government benefits.

This plan has several pitfalls. Consider what would happen if you gave your son's or daughter's inheritance to your non-disabled child to hold and:

- Your non-disabled child files for divorce, and his or her spouse claims a share of the money
- Your non-disabled child has creditor problems and is sued

- Your non-disabled child gets into a financial bind and needs the money for medical bills, mortgage payments, or his or her own child's tuition
- Your non-disabled child dies first. If that were to occur, your child's funds would become part of your non-disabled child's estate and probably pass to the surviving spouse or children.

What can you do to avoid these potential problems?

To protect your son or daughter with a disability, leave some of your property to a special needs trust. (See Chapter 23, "Using a Special Needs Trust to Plan Your Estate.") With a properly worded trust, your son or daughter can have money in the trust and still qualify for most government programs that require a person to be poor. The trust funds can be used to pay for items and services that are not provided by any public benefit program.

It is true that a special needs trust can be rather restrictive, and the trustee must be careful about how he or she spends money from the trust. As I explained in Chapter 8, "Supplementing SSI," the trustee should not give a beneficiary who gets SSI any cash, food, or housing items. But if the trustee is careful to observe the rules, the public benefits can remain intact, and your son's or daughter's life will be enriched.

What if there is no one to act as the trustee? In that case, you could consider leaving your son's or daughter's inheritance to a *pooled trust*. Currently in Massachusetts, two non-profit organizations operate these kinds of trusts. For a modest fee, these trusts offer professional management, oversight by staff who understand the complexities of public benefit programs, and even case management and social work services. Chapter 23, "Using a Special Needs Trust to Plan Your Estate," covers pooled trusts.

21

Estate Planning Basics for Special Families

Topics include

**Avoid leaving a direct inheritance to a
son or daughter with a disability
Three kinds of ownership
Planning with life insurance and retirement accounts**

Now that you know what could happen if you don't plan ahead, I hope you will be motivated to get started. The following chapters explain how to build a sound estate plan using wills and trusts. Before reading about them, however, you need to understand some basic concepts in estate planning. These include the importance of how you own your property, and why you must be careful to name the proper beneficiaries for your life insurance and retirement accounts. There is also a ten-step plan to get you started.

Do Not Leave Property Directly to Your Minor Children or Your Child with a Disability

In the previous chapter, I advised you not to leave any money or property directly to your son or daughter with a disability. Now I will repeat that advice, because it is one of the fundamental principles of planning when there is a child with a disability. Unless only a small amount of money is involved ($2,000 or less), your son or daughter should not own any money in his or her own name. To protect your son's or daughter's financial interests, you should prepare an estate plan that includes a special needs trust.

The advice to not leave a direct inheritance to a son or daughter with a disability also applies to your children without disabilities. As I explained in the previous chapter, a child who inherits any property in Massachusetts may be entitled to receive that property outright—with no strings attached—at age eighteen. This is also true if a life insurance policy or retirement account names a minor child as the beneficiary. When a parent dies, the insurance company or retirement plan administrator will release the funds to the child's surviving parent or to a conservator. (A conservator is a person appointed by the Court to manage funds that belong to a minor or a person with a disability.) When the child reaches age 18, the conservator *must* hand over the funds.

If you want to restrict your child's access to the money beyond age 18, you must use a trust. This could be a testamentary trust that is written into your will or a revocable trust that is separate from your will. Both kinds of trust are discussed later in this section.

Who Will Receive Your Property Depends on How You Own It

Before I meet with a client to prepare an estate plan, I ask him or her to prepare a list of family assets that describes how those assets are owned. I also ask the client to review the beneficiaries of all life insurance and retirement accounts. It is important to gather this information when you begin to plan your estate. Since a major focus of planning often involves creating trusts for minor children and children with disabilities, you need to make sure that, on your death, your assets will get into the hands of the trustee. How that will occur depends in part on how you own your assets:

- Assets that you own in your own name will either pass under your will or, if you have no valid will, to your legal heirs according to the laws in your state.
- Any jointly owned assets will pass to the surviving joint owner.
- Assets for which you have named a beneficiary will pass to that beneficiary. (See the insert later in this chapter.)

With all these different kinds of ownership, you need to make sure that your assets are correctly titled. Otherwise, on your death, your property might not go where you intended. One important part of planning in this area involves naming the proper beneficiaries.

Estate Planning with Assets that Have Beneficiaries

If you are like a lot of people, you might not pay much attention to your assets that have beneficiaries named. When you bought a life insurance policy or set up a new retirement account at work, you may have quickly filled in a beneficiary's name without giving much though to what you wrote. This is unfortunate, because your family's beneficiary designated assets could easily amount to several hundred thousand dollars. That figure could even be higher when all the potential death benefits from life insurance are taken into account. But even if you only have a modest amount of life insurance or a small retirement account, you still need to plan properly. Here are some important points to keep in mind.

Name the proper beneficiary

It is important to name the proper beneficiary. Let's say that you want your minor children and your child with a disability to receive your assets through a trust. You must name the trust—not your children—to receive the proceeds of the policy. If you put your son's or daughter's name on the beneficiary form, the company will pay the funds directly to your child. This could cause financial hardship for your child with a disability and impose unnecessary administrative costs on your estate. To illustrate:

> A young man (age 25) with disabilities inherited a small life insurance policy from his mother. Before she died, the mother had signed a will and special needs trust. But she overlooked a critical step: she named her son—not his trust—to receive her life insurance policy.
>
> After she died, the insurance company made

the check payable directly to her son. As a result, he no longer qualified for SSI and MassHealth. In order to re-establish eligibility for those programs, the insurance money had to be transferred to a trust. A legal guardian had to be appointed, and the court had to approve the transfer. The legal costs to achieve this were substantial.

Three Kinds of Ownership

Sole ownership. Sole ownership refers to assets you own in your own name. On your death, these individually owned assets pass under your will. If you do not have a valid will, they will pass to your legal heirs according to your state's laws.

Joint ownership. Joint ownership means assets that you own together with another person. Most married couples own their assets as joint tenants with rights of survivorship. These assets pass automatically to the surviving co-owner. If you and your spouse own an asset jointly, your spouse will become the sole owner immediately on your death.

Assets that pass to others by beneficiary designation. These are assets such as life insurance, retirement accounts, and annuities. When you take out a life insurance policy or set up a retirement account, you can name one or more primary beneficiaries and one or more secondary beneficiaries. On your death, the proceeds will pass directly to the beneficiary you have named to receive them. If you do not name a beneficiary, the insurance contract or plan documents determine who will receive the asset. Most companies will give the assets to your surviving spouse, if you have one, otherwise to your children.

Retirement plans can be taxing

If you name your son's or daughter's trust to receive your retirement accounts on your death, that could cause income taxes to increase. This could occur if the trust is not properly worded. As a result, the trust might have to pay more income taxes than an individual would owe.

It is difficult to generalize about this, because there are so many different kinds of retirement accounts, including traditional IRAs, Roth IRAs, 401(k)s, and profit sharing plans. These accounts all have their own rules, and the tax laws that govern them are quite complicated. To be on the safe side, be sure to review the wording of the trust with a qualified attorney before you proceed. In that way, you can be assured that your son or daughter will receive the maximum possible financial benefit from your retirement accounts.

Do not forget to disinherit your former spouse

If you are divorced, don't forget to remove your former spouse from your life insurance and retirement accounts. If you don't, the insurer or plan administrator will pay the benefits to your ex. This will occur even if you have severed your legal ties and changed your will. To illustrate:

> A single parent with two children re-married and made her new husband the beneficiary of her life insurance policy. Later, the couple separated but never bothered to get divorced.

> When the woman died several years later, her children were dismayed to learn that their stepfather would receive the life insurance proceeds. Despite their best efforts, they could not persuade him to "do the right thing." The children, who had no legal recourse, received nothing.

Timing can be important when it comes to dealing with a former spouse. In Massachusetts, if you are going through a divorce, you cannot remove your spouse's name from certain kinds of assets, including life insurance policies and retirement accounts, without court permission. Such permission is required after a divorce has been filed and before the divorce has become final.

A Coordinated Plan Works Best

Thus far, I have stressed that you need properly worded estate planning documents. But you also need to coordinate the ownership of your assets—especially your assets that have beneficiaries—with those documents. Let's look at the ways that a coordinated plan can help achieve some common estate planning goals.

Protect public benefits for a child with a disability

Parents of children with disabilities usually want to both protect the child's funds and preserve eligibility for public benefits. To accomplish this, the first step is to have your lawyer create a special needs trust. (See Chapter 23, "Using a Special Needs Trust to Plan Your Estate.")

> You want your life insurance policy to go to your child's special needs trust. For that to occur, you must name your child's trust as the beneficiary of your policy. Remember, don't name your child as the beneficiary. If you do, the company will give the proceeds directly to your son or daughter instead of the trust.

Postpone an inheritance for a child without a disability

Many parents don't want their minor children to receive their entire inheritance until they reach a mature age, such as 25.

> You are setting up a new retirement account at work. You want your spouse to receive the funds if he or she is living on your death; otherwise, you want your children to receive the funds at

age 25. Your lawyer writes a will and trust to that effect.

To ensure that your children will receive the funds through the trust, you must name the trust to be the alternate beneficiary. If you don't, the company will pay the proceeds directly to your children's guardian, not the trustee, and your children can have the money outright at age 18.

Benefit a first family

Some parents have remarried and want to leave some property to their children from a previous marriage.

You want your children from your first marriage to receive some of your property. However, you own all your assets jointly with your current spouse, and you have named him or her as the primary beneficiary of your life insurance and retirement accounts. On your death, all those assets will pass automatically to your spouse. Whether your first family gets anything will depend entirely on your spouse's generosity, because he or she is under no legal obligation to take care of them.

What can you do instead? Consider leaving your first family a beneficiary designated asset, such as a life insurance policy.

Give peace of mind to single parents

Some single parents want their own parents or sibling to hold their children's property after they are gone. These parents don't want their former spouse or partner to get control of their children's inheritance.

You want your mother to manage your children's property and use it for their support and education. You have put your property in joint names with your mother and made her the beneficiary of your life insurance policy, all with the understanding that she will use the property for your children. But this arrangement may not necessarily safeguard your children's property. On your death, your mother will own your property outright, but she might have to use it to pay her own bills, including nursing home costs.

To protect your children's money, you should create a trust and name the trust to receive your life insurance. You can make your mother the trustee. Then re-title your property either in your own name or the name of the trust. That way, your children's funds will be kept separate from your mother's property.

Ten Steps to Sound Planning

Are you ready to start the estate planning process but not sure where to begin? Here is a ten-step plan to get you started:

Step 1: Choose a qualified professional

Select a qualified attorney or financial advisor to work with you and set up a meeting. The professional you choose should be experienced in his or her field and knowledgeable about public benefits and disabilities.

Step 2: Make an inventory of your assets, paying special attention to how they are titled, including beneficiary designations

Taking stock of what you own is important. An inventory shows how much property you have to pass on. But as I explained earlier, *how* you own your assets is important too, because that will determine who receives your property on your death. Your attorney will need this information in order to properly coordinate your individually titled property, jointly owned assets, and beneficiary designated assets (life insurance and retirement accounts) with your estate planning documents.

Step 3: Establish your goals

There is no one-size-fits-all estate plan. Your goals will be as unique as your family. Some typical goals of a family that includes a child with a disability might be to:

- Protect the long-term interests of your child with special needs
- Ensure that your children without disabilities can afford higher education
- Choose an appropriate age for your children without disabilities to receive their inheritance
- Leave enough money for your spouse to live comfortably
- Protect your assets from creditors
- Reduce or eliminate excessive probate costs
- Reduce or eliminate any potential estate taxes

Step 4: Prioritize your goals

Since you probably don't have unlimited funds to spend on estate planning services, you may need to scale back or prioritize your goals. Your choices might be influenced by factors such as your age, earnings, asset level, and health. A healthy young couple would probably emphasize saving for college over reducing estate taxes, while an older couple with adult children might focus on eliminating estate taxes and probate costs. Your attorney or financial advisor can help you prioritize your goals.

Step 5: Identify the people who will carry out your wishes

You must identify the people who will raise your minor children and make important decisions for them (the legal guardians). You must also select trustees to manage your child's special needs trust and your non-disabled children's inheritances until they can be distributed. Last, you must select an executor and an alternate executor to settle your estate.

Step 6: Purchase any necessary insurance

Purchase any necessary life, disability, or long-term care insurance through your financial planner or insurance agent. Take special care to make the appropriate beneficiary designations for life insurance accounts (see below).

Step 7: Complete the estate planning documents

Have your attorney draft the necessary estate planning documents. These will most likely include a will, special needs trust, durable power of attorney, health care proxy, living will, and perhaps one or more additional trusts. When the documents are in final form, meet with your attorney to have them properly signed, witnessed, and notarized.

Step 8: Coordinate the beneficiary designations with your overall estate plan

Have your attorney prepare the correct language for all beneficiary designated assets, such as life insurance policies, retirement accounts, and annuity contracts. Then contact each insurance company or retirement plan administrator to update the beneficiary forms. Follow up to make sure that the company has implemented your instructions. Often this can be done online.

Step 9: Communicate your wishes

Give signed copies of your legal documents to your executor and trustee. Tell them where to find the original documents as well as other important papers such as bank account statements and life insurance policies.

Step 10: Monitor your estate plan

Plan to periodically review your estate plan to assure that it still meets your goals. A good time to do this is after the birth of a child, on a child's graduation or emancipation, or on your or your spouse's retirement. Your estate plan might also need a second look if there have been any significant changes in the laws that relate to your situation, such as Medicaid, income tax, or estate tax laws.

22

Using a Will to Plan Your Estate

Topics include

Postponing an inheritance for a child with a disability
Guardians
Executors
Communicating your personal wishes
for a son's or daughter's care

Now that you are familiar with the basic principles of estate planning for special families, we can turn to the specific documents you will need. The first one is a will. If you are a single person, you should have a will. A will lets you control how your assets will be disposed of on your death. It also allows you to nominate guardians for your minor children and for an adult son or daughter with a disability.

Wills are also important for married couples, even if both partners own all their assets in joint names. If you and your spouse both die at the same time, a will can ensure that your children receive your assets according to your wishes—instead of at age 18—and that your son or daughter with a disability will be protected.

The Contents of a Will

When I interview a client for a will, here are some of the questions I ask.

At what age do you want your children without disabilities to receive their inheritances?

As I explained earlier, when a minor child inherits property in

Massachusetts, the court usually appoints a conservator to manage the child's property. That person's job is to manage the inheritance until the child reaches adulthood (age 18). When the child reaches age 18, however, the conservator *must* release the child's inheritance directly to him or her.

The age of distribution can sometimes be delayed to age 21 if the conservator takes special steps through the court to do so. But attorney's fees and court costs can make this an expensive proposition. Moreover, in most parents' view, 21 is not much better than 18, especially if the child is immature or significant amounts of money are involved.

One way to avoid these problems is to include a *testamentary trust* in your will. That way, your children will not receive their inheritance until they reach the age that you selected when you wrote the trust. You can pick one age, such as 25, or have staggered distributions, such as one-half at age 25 and the rest at age 30. In the meantime, the trustee you selected can invest the children's money and dole it out for worthwhile purposes you specified when you wrote the trust. These could include education, medical care, purchasing a home, or starting a business.

Another option is to set up an *unfunded revocable trust* for your children. Unlike a testamentary trust, a revocable trust is separate from your will and requires little if any court oversight. Chapter 26, "Beyond the Basics," discusses these trusts.

Who do you want to raise your minor children?

When both parents die, or if one parent dies and the surviving parent is absent or unavailable, the court will appoint one or more guardians and conservators for the minor (under age 18) children. The *guardian's* job is to raise the children and make decisions for them involving their education, religious training, and medical care.

If the children have inherited any money, a *conservator* will probably be appointed. The conservator's job is to handle the children's funds until they reach age 18 (or 21 at the latest, as explained earlier in this chapter).

Sometimes a dispute can arise if the surviving family members do not see eye to eye on who can best fulfill the guardian or conservator role. Then costly litigation can ensue. The result could be that the relative you would least want to raise your children or manage their funds might end up in control.

Instead of leaving your minor children to an uncertain fate, you can write a will in which you nominate a guardian and conservator for them. You can name one person for both roles, or you can name different people. The people you select do not become guardians and conservators automatically; they still have to apply to the court to be appointed. While there is no guarantee that the people you select will be the ones the court chooses, your expressed preferences will most likely control the outcome.

Who do you want to be the guardian for your adult son or daughter with a disability?

If you and your spouse are already the guardians for your adult son or daughter with a disability, then on your death, your spouse can continue to serve as the guardian. But when both of you are gone, there may be some uncertainty about who should take over. You can remove any uncertainty by naming one or more people in your will. Unless the person is clearly unfit to serve, the Court must appoint him or her.

Will you divide your property equally among your children?

Most married couples want their surviving spouse to receive their individually owned property. However, as I explained in the previous chapter, if there is no valid will, a person's individually owned property will pass to both the surviving spouse and the children. In order to make sure your spouse will receive all your individually owned property, you must have a will.

What would you want to happen to your property when you and your spouse are both gone? An issue some parents struggle with is whether to divide their assets equally among their children (including their child with a disability) or in some other proportion. There is no right or wrong answer to this question; it depends entirely on your family's circumstances.

In some families, the parents decide to leave more to the child who does not have a disability. These parents reason that he or she can make better use of the money by paying for higher education, buying a home, or getting started in a business. Other families will consider the same set of circumstances and arrive at a different conclusion—the child with a disability should get more because his or her needs are greater.

Do you want a particular person to have your personal effects?

Most of us own personal effects such as clothing, jewelry, china, and household furnishings. Most people are content to leave that kind of property to a spouse or children to share as they see fit. However, some people want to earmark family heirlooms or items with sentimental value for a particular family member.

A will allows you to do that. You could mention each item in your will. A better approach, however, is to write a side letter (also called a memorandum) that is separate from your will. The side letter can list each item and name the person you want to receive it. If your wishes change (or you give away any property or acquire any new items), you don't have to formally update your will. A paragraph in your will instructs your executor to comply with the written side letter.

A side letter is not strictly subject to court oversight, nor is your executor necessarily bound to follow your instructions. This is because in most cases the side letter is not executed with the formalities of a will. (It is not properly witnessed and notarized.) However, since the executor was presumably selected with his or her trustworthiness in mind, most likely he or she will adhere to your wishes.

Who do you want to settle your estate?

You can name one or more executors to carry out your estate plan. The court must appoint the person you select unless he or she is obviously unfit to serve.

An executor has several clearly defined responsibilities, including:

- Locate your will and file it with the probate court
- Inventory and preserve your property
- Pay your bills and taxes
- Distribute your assets according to the instructions in your will

- Provide financial accounts to the court and to your heirs that show how your assets were distributed

Most couples name their surviving husband or wife to act as the executor. You should nominate an alternate executor in case your spouse is not available. You can name one or more individuals, who can be family members, friends, or professionals.

What qualities should you look for in an executor? The executor does not necessarily need to have any special expertise in law or finance because in most cases, he or she will hire an attorney to assist with the administrative tasks. Probably the most important qualities to consider are trustworthiness, organization, and compatibility with your other family members.

What Information Does Not Belong in a Will?

Perhaps you want to be buried in particular cemetery plot or be cremated and have your ashes spread in a beautiful place. If so, should these kinds of instructions be included in your will? No, say most experts. By the time your will has been located, the surviving family members could have already made arrangements that are contrary to your wishes. And if there is a disagreement among surviving family members, decisions about final arrangements can't be postponed until the court can act.

But this is not to say that your funeral and burial instructions should not be written down. It's just that they do not necessarily belong in your will. Instead, consider using a memorandum that is separate from your will. A benefit to this approach is that you can revise the memorandum if your wishes change over time.

Make two copies of the memorandum and keep one copy with your will and the other copy with your important papers. Most importantly, don't forget to discuss your wishes with your family. That way, you can be assured that your wishes will be honored even if your will is not yet operative.

Limitations of a Will

As important as a will is, there are some things it cannot accomplish:

- A will does not let you avoid probate costs and delays and reduce estate taxes. To do that, you will need to use one or more of the trust arrangements discussed in Chapter 26, "Beyond the Basics."
- A will does not control assets that you own with others or that have beneficiaries. A will only controls assets that you own in your name alone. It does not apply to any jointly owned property or beneficiary controlled assets such as annuities, life insurance policies, and retirement accounts. To plan effectively, you must coordinate these assets with your overall estate planning goals.
- A will does not help if you become disabled and cannot effectively manage your property. Since a will does not take effect until your death, it will not help you if you become disabled and need help to manage your property. To plan for the possibility of your own incapacity, you should consider signing a durable power of attorney, health care directive, living will, and perhaps even a revocable living trust. Chapter 25, "Planning for Your Own Incapacity," discusses these documents.
- You cannot use a will to communicate your personal wishes for your special needs son's or daughter's care after you are gone. You could make your wishes known with a side letter or a letter of intent. Chapter 24, "Communicating Your Personal Instructions for Your Son's or Daughter's Care," discusses both of these documents.

23

Using a Special Needs Trust to Plan Your Estate

Topics include

Trustees
Remainder beneficiaries
Special needs trusts
Pooled trusts

In the previous chapters, I encouraged you to leave some of your property to your son or daughter with a disability instead of disinheriting him or her. This chapter explains how to leave an inheritance through a special needs trust. I also explain pooled trusts, which can be an alternative to a special needs trust.

How Does a Special Needs Trust Operate?

When there is a child with a disability in the family, parents often recognize that the child will need lifetime care. That can easily cost tens of thousands of dollars a year when you take into account housing, staff supervision, day programs, employment supports, transportation, and medical care. Since few of us can afford these costs, we must seek help from public benefit programs.

A special needs trust is a way that a person with a disability can receive an inheritance and still obtain public benefits. The trust funds can be used to pay for the items and services that are not covered by any public benefit programs. The trust assets are intended to enhance the beneficiary's quality of life, not provide basic support. However, if the beneficiary does not receive any public benefits, the trust funds could be used for the beneficiary's day-to-day needs.

Personalizing a Special Needs Trust

There is no single "form" trust that will fit everyone's needs. A special needs trust must be tailored to your family's particular situation. Before your attorney can prepare your special needs trust, he or she will need you to make some key decisions. You will need to:

Select the remainder beneficiaries

When you create a special needs trust, you can choose who will receive any assets that may be left in the trust when your special needs child passes on. These *remainder beneficiaries* can be other family members, such as your other children. Alternatively, you can let your son or daughter with a disability specify who will receive the unspent funds. He or she can do this by writing a will. (This is called a *power of appointment*). The will can name friends, relatives, or even favorite charities.

Identify successor trustees

In most cases, you (the parent) will be the trustee while you are living (*initial trustee*). When you are gone (or if you cannot serve due to disability or for other reasons), one or more *successor trustees* will take over managing the trust.

The trustees' primary duties are to invest the trust funds so that they earn a reasonable rate of return, keep accurate financial records of the trust, and handle tax reporting. In most cases, the trustees will have "sole discretion" to decide how the trust funds will be used. This means that only the trustee—not the beneficiary—can make investment and spending decisions.

Most parents choose one or more of their children without disabilities to be the *successor trustee*. This makes sense because the children without disabilities usually know their sibling best and can make the soundest choices. You should be aware, however, that choosing a sibling as the trustee may create a potential conflict of interest if your child without disabilities is also the remainder beneficiary. Some skeptics might ask, if the child has a personal financial stake in the trust, will he or she be motivated to spend money on the special needs sibling?

This is not to say that siblings should not be chosen. In fact, most parents who are cautioned about this potential conflict of interest choose to overlook it. They believe that the child's love and affection for the special needs sibling will prevail. If your child's potential self-interest is a concern, you can name an *independent co-trustee*. That could be a person who is not a blood relative of your son or daughter and has no personal financial stake in the trust. The independent co-trustee could be either an organization such as a bank or an individual such as an attorney or financial advisor. Another option could be to use one of the pooled trust arrangements described later in this chapter.

Two Kinds of Special Needs Trusts

There are two different kinds of special needs trusts: *self-funded* (also called *self-settled*) trusts and *third party* trusts. There are important differences between the two kinds of trusts.

One difference is the source of the funds. A *self-funded special needs trust* contains property such as an inheritance, gift, or the proceeds of a personal injury settlement that originally belonged to the beneficiary with a disability. By contrast, a *third party special needs trust* contains the assets of someone other than the beneficiary with a disability, such as a parent or grandparent. That person leaves his or her own property to a third party trust for the beneficiary. The property can be transferred during the person's lifetime or at death under a will, life insurance policy, or retirement account.

Another important difference is what happens to any property that is left in the trust when the beneficiary with a disability dies. Most *self-funded trusts* state that any remaining funds must be used to reimburse the state for the beneficiary's Medicaid bill. This is required by the current SSI law.

Most *third party trusts* state that any remaining funds will go to the beneficiary's relatives. An exception could occur if the person who creates the trust needs to qualify for public benefits himself or herself. A common situation involves a parent who needs nursing home care but cannot qualify financially for Medicaid because he or she has too many assets. In that case, the parent can transfer his or her excess resources to a third party trust for a son or daughter with a disability. (The trust benefits the child, not the parent). The trust must state that when the child dies, any remaining funds will be used to reimburse the state for the child's (not the parent's) Medicaid bill.

Consider a corporate or professional trustee

When there is no sibling or family member to act as trustee, a corporate or professional trustee could be employed. A corporate trustee is a bank or trust company that serves as trustee for many trusts. Professional trustees may include law firms or individual attorneys and financial planners who have experience managing trusts.

A professional trustee can avoid the potential conflict of interest that is inherent in having a sibling act as the trustee. Professional trustees can offer other advantages too, such as professional management and investment expertise. The trust departments are experienced in handling investments, tax filings, and accountings. Another benefit is longevity. A corporate trustee can provide management over the beneficiary's lifetime, even after other family members have passed on.

However, finding a bank or trust company that will take on a special needs trust can be a daunting task. Most financial institutions in the greater Boston area currently require an initial funding of at least $500,000, and many are not interested at all if the beneficiary has a disability and public benefits are involved. Administrative costs can also be a drawback. Banks generally charge more for their services than individual trustees. They may also hire an expert consultant to advise on any public benefit issues. The consultant's costs are billed separately to the trust and may add up to a prohibitive sum.

How much do professional trustees charge? Professional trustees usually set their fees on a sliding scale according to the amount of assets under investment. For example, for a $500,000 trust, the annual fee might be $5,000 (1.0% of the trust's market value). The trustee's fee would include preparing annual accounts and tax filings. However, if the trustee provides any legal services (such as representing the beneficiary in any Social Security related matters), these services may be charged separately in addition to the trustee's normal fees.

By contrast, most non-professional trustees, including family members, charge an hourly rate for their services. The trustee's hourly rate will depend on the person's skills and background as well as the actual services being performed. A trustee with a financial services background might charge an hourly rate commensurate with his or her skills, such as $50 to $75 per hour. However, a trustee without financial or even bookkeeping skills might charge only $15 to $20 per hour. Similarly, when the trustee meets with a tax advisor or attorney, they usually charge a higher hourly rate than when they make a bank deposit. Additional costs such as accountant, tax preparer, and attorney's fees are usually billed separately.

Nominate a family member and a bank to serve as co-trustees

Another approach is to have a family member and a professional trustee (bank or trust company) serve together as co-trustees. The family member (the "personal trustee") keeps in touch with the beneficiary and decides how the money should be spent. The bank or trust company ("financial trustee") is in charge of investing the trust funds.

If the beneficiary needs money, the personal trustee tells the financial trustee to send a check. The personal trustee should have the ability to remove the financial trustee and replace it with another bank or trust company.

Select a way to choose additional successor trustees

Let's say you and your spouse are the initial trustees, and your children without disabilities are the successor trustees. What would happen if your son or daughter outlives both you and the siblings? Who would be the trustee then? Thinking about what could happen in the distant future can be worrisome. If your son or daughter lives long enough, his or her financial well-being could be in the hands of someone you have never met.

Planning for the distant future can alleviate some of the worry you have now. Even if you cannot necessarily control *who* the successor trustee will be, you can at least put a mechanism in place for selecting a responsible person. The trust can specify that the successor trustee will be chosen by:

- The trustee who is resigning
- The remaining co-trustee (if there is one)
- The beneficiary (although he or she could not be the trustee, and the choice could be vetoed by one or more family members)
- A committee composed of the beneficiary's nearest relatives

- An organization such as the local Arc
- The probate and family court that has jurisdiction over the trust

There is no right or wrong way to choose the successor trustee. You can even be creative and devise an arrangement that is unique to your family. And remember that if your family's circumstances change over time, you can usually amend the trustee provisions to meet your needs.

Trust Terms

Account: A financial summary of the trust's activity for a specific period of time, usually a year

Beneficiary: A person who benefits from a trust

Grantor: The person who creates the trust, sometimes called a donor, settlor, or trustor

Irrevocable trust: A trust that cannot be changed

Living trust: A trust that is in existence while the donor is alive, also called an *inter vivos* trust

Revocable trust: A trust that the grantor can change while he or she is living

Testamentary trust: A trust that is included in a person's will and takes effect on his or her death

Trust: An arrangement in which one person holds property for the benefit of another person (the beneficiary)

Consider a committee approach

Another approach is to use a committee to manage a special needs trust. The committee can be composed of the beneficiary's relatives, close friends, an attorney or social work professional, or a combination of these individuals. The committee functions like a watchdog, performing important functions like overseeing investments, deciding on distributions, and reviewing the trustee's financial accounts. The committee could appoint and remove trustees and choose successors. A committee approach can be helpful when there are conflicts in the family or when there is no single individual who can serve as the trustee.

Decide when the trust will be funded

Do you think you might use the special needs trust right away? If so, be sure to tell your attorney about your plans at the initial meeting, before he or she prepares the trust. A special needs trust that is going to become operational right away will probably be different than one that will not be used for many years in the future. To avoid any misunderstandings, make sure that your attorney is aware of your plans.

Most parents intend that the special needs will not begin to operate until they pass on. At that time, the trust can receive the property they have earmarked for the child with a disability. A portion or their estates, life insurance benefits, and retirement assets will flow into the trust. Until that occurs, however, the document will simply be put away with the other estate planning paperwork until it is needed—most likely, not for many years in the future.

However, some parents want to use the trust right away as a way to save money for the child with a disability. Grandparents and other family members may want to contribute by making cash gifts or naming the trust to receive a portion of their estates. When the trust actually receives property—it has been "funded"—parents plan to invest the trust monies in stocks, bonds, and mutual funds.

Funding the trust while you are still living may seem appealing, but there can be some drawbacks.

- A funded special needs trust should be irrevocable. That means that after the funds have been transferred to the trustee, you cannot make any changes to the trust document, even if your family circumstances change. And, of course, you couldn't change your mind, cancel the trust, and take the money back.
- Tax preparation fees could increase. This is because the trust must use a separate employer identification (EIN) number assigned by the Internal Revenue Service. (The child's Social Security Number should not be used.) When there is a separate EIN, the trust must file its own income tax return every year.
- Income taxes could increase. The trust tax rates are higher than the tax rates for individuals. Depending on how the trust is written and the amount of earnings, the amount of income taxes the trust would pay might make saving through the trust prohibitive.

In short, if you think you might want to use your special needs trust as a savings fund, be sure to discuss your plans with your attorney. There might be better ways to save money for your son or daughter with a disability. Some of them are discussed in Chapter 28, "Money Matters."

Pooled Trusts: An Alternative to a Special Needs Trust

For some families, a special needs trust is not an option. No friend or family member is available to act as the trustee, and there is not enough money to attract a corporate or professional trustee. A satisfactory solution could be third party pooled trust. Currently two non-profit organizations operate third party pooled trusts in Massachusetts. They are the PLAN of Massachusetts, Inc., and Jewish Family and Children's Services (JF&CS). For contact information for both organizations, see the Appendix.

How a pooled trust operates

In a pooled trust arrangement, the members' contributions are combined (pooled) for investment and management purposes. However, each member has his or her own account. The member's funds are used for items like clothes, recreation, travel, special therapies, and one-on-one staff assistance. These items are specified when the member's account is opened.

If any funds remain in the account when the member dies, they can pass to other family members who were designated when the trust account was established.[14]

Benefits of a pooled trust

Pooled trusts have many benefits:

- Peace of mind. It can be comforting to know that your son's or daughter's interests will be safeguarded by a qualified social services agency when you are no longer there to help.
- Accountability. Because the agency provides oversight and its employees are bonded and insured, you can be confident that the funds will be properly managed and accounted for. This might not be the case if you must rely on family members.
- Longevity. If your son or daughter with a disability outlives the rest of your family, the pooled trust can provide continuous financial oversight for his or her lifetime.

---

14 This is *not* the case with another kind of pooled trust that is called a first party pooled trust or (d)(4)(C) trust. These first party trusts generally contain funds that belonged to the person with a disability before they were put in the trust. When the person with a disability dies, 10% to 15% of the funds are retained by the trust and used to assist other members. The remaining funds are used to repay the state for the person's Medicaid benefits. There are currently three first party trusts in Massachusetts: The MARC Trust, operated by the PLAN of Massachusetts, Inc.; the Berkshire County Arc Master Special Needs Pooled Trust; and Family Service of Greater Boston Pooled Trust. There is contact information for these trusts in the Appendix.

24

Communicating Personal Instructions for a Son's or Daughter's Care

Topics include

Directions book
Side letter
Letter of intent

We parents know our children better than anyone else. After all, we are the ones who feed them, nurse them when they are sick, and generally care for them day in and day out. But as indispensable as we are, there are times when we must turn over our children's care to others, such as babysitters, nurses, and respite providers. And in the long term, it is possible that our children may outlive us. Someday someone else will permanently take over their care. This raises the question: What do we want caregivers to know?

Whether you are planning for an evening out or a lengthier absence, you must consider many different kinds of information. For the short-term, there is practical information on topics like medications, allergies, proper emergency care, etc. You will also want to describe your son or daughter personal habits, including eating and sleeping patterns, food preferences, and any behavior issues. And when it comes to long-term planning, you probably want to convey your wishes for your son's or daughter's future care. You might want your son or daughter to continue to live in your home after you are gone. Or you might want him or her to take an annual vacation someplace warm. Or perhaps your son or daughter does not do well with an overly rigid behavior plan, and you do not want him or her to be subjected to one.

Whether you are focused on the Great Beyond or just the Here and

Now, it is important to write everything down. In that way, caregivers will know what they are supposed to do. When it comes to conveying important information, you do not need to use any particular format. The rest of this chapter gives three options to consider.

Directions Book

When it comes to organizing factual information like your son's or daughter's schedule, medical treatments, and important contacts, many parents like *Directions: Resources for Your Child's Care.* This comprehensive organizing tool is available from the Massachusetts Department of Public Health, Division of Perinatal, Early Childhood, and Special Needs. It has ten chapters and a monthly calendar to write down important dates and appointments. You download the forms and keep them together in a three-ring binder. The book includes sections for health records, school records, doctor and hospital contact information, and health insurance. In another section, you can place information and resources for taking care of your child's daily needs, such as health care services you use at home. For information about obtaining this book, see the Resources section.

Side Letter to the Special Needs Trust

While providing factual is information, many parents want to go further. They want to express their personal wishes for a son's and daughter's care after they are gone. Even if you have prepared a special needs trust, that document may not go far enough in describing your wishes. In fact, many parents have told me that the special needs trust can seem quite dry and impersonal. And they're right—it is!

A typical special needs trust gives the trustee general directions about how to spend the trust funds in ways that will not interfere with the beneficiary's public benefits. There may even be a list of permitted items like vacations, hobbies, sports equipment, and tickets to events. Certainly it is important to tell the trustee what he or she *can* use the trust funds for. But most parents also want to tell the trustee what he or she *should* spend the money on.

This kind of personal information is not usually included in most special needs trusts. There are two main reasons:

- Updates and ease of revisions. Since a special needs trust is a legal document, any change must be signed, notarized, and properly incorporated into the trust document. However, you probably do not want to visit your lawyer every time your wishes change—that could be time consuming and expensive.
- The trustee's flexibility. A trustee must be able to respond to your son's or daughter's circumstances at any particular time. What you specify for your son or daughter at age seven might not necessarily be what is appropriate—or what your son or daughter wants—at age twenty-seven.

A side letter can be a solution to this dilemma. A side letter can go hand-in-hand with your special needs trust. You can use a side letter to give detailed personal instructions to the trustee about how you want the trust funds to be spent.

Since the side letter does not need to be witnessed or notarized, you can update it whenever your wishes change. You just write a new letter, place it with the special needs trust, and give a copy to your trustee and anyone else you want to have the letter. Don't forget to tear up the old letter and tell the trustee that you have replaced it.

Can you be absolutely sure that the trustee will abide by your wishes? Frankly, no. Since the side letter is not actually part of the special needs trust, the trustee is not legally bound to follow it. Still, you should not let this deter you. If you write a side letter that clearly states your wishes and instructions, the trustee will probably feel morally obligated to comply with it. If he or she does not, this could be grounds to have the trustee removed by someone acting on your child's behalf, such as a legal guardian.

Letter of Intent

Another way to impart personal information is through a letter of intent. You can include anything you want future caregivers to know about your son or daughter. Here are some kinds of information you may want to consider:

- Basic factual information like your son's or daughter's date and place of birth, Social Security Number, religion, place of residence, and place of work
- Likes and dislikes, including food, recreation, hobbies, interests, and kinds of environments
- Important people, including names and addresses of siblings, special relatives, people your son or daughter especially likes, guardians, trustees, advocates, representative payee, and power of attorney (if any)
- Medical information, including diagnoses, level of functioning, vision, hearing, speech, mobility, medication, allergies, operations, and recent testing
- Names, addresses, and telephone numbers of regular physicians, dentists, therapists, and specialists
- A particular church, synagogue, or mosque that your son or daughter prefers to attend
- What works well for your son or daughter, including current and past school programs, living arrangements, work, education strategies, and approaches to learning
- Your perspective on your son's or daughter's capabilities in terms of education, employment, and social relationships
- An overview of your child's life and your vision for his or her future
- Anything else you want future caregivers to know about your son or daughter
- Final arrangements for your son or daughter, including your preference for cremation or burial, location of the plot, any pre-paid arrangements, and specific instructions

After your have written your letter of intent, sign and date it. Then give a copy to your son's or daughter's future caregivers. Last, don't forget to periodically update the letter of intent, perhaps annually, to reflect any changes in your son's or daughter's circumstances.

Since a letter of intent is a personal document, you do not have to follow any particular format. I like the Special Letter of Intent kit that is included with *The Special Needs Planning Guide* (listed in the Resources section). Another resource is the Footprints for the Future document, which is available from the Arc of East Middlesex in Reading, Massachusetts (http://www.theemarc.org).

25

Planning for Your Own Incapacity

Topics include

Durable Power of Attorney
Health care proxy
Living will
Special needs "payback" trust

Most of us have plans for a long, healthy life. We intend to enjoy our retirement, play with our grandchildren, and oversee the care of our adult child with a disability as long as possible. But the difficult reality is that some of us will suffer a disability that is serious enough to interfere with our day-to-day functioning. If that happened to you, how would you get by? Who would take care of you? How would your bills be paid? If you needed long-term care, would your assets be depleted by paying for nursing home costs? And if that happened, could you meet your financial commitments to your son or daughter with a disability?

None of us like to think about these difficult questions. Yet it can be reassuring to know that we have consciously considered the worst-case scenario and arranged our affairs if that should occur. In this chapter, I discuss some practical strategies to plan for the possibility that you might become disabled. Three routine, inexpensive planning documents can help you avoid guardianship and conservatorship. A financial planner can assess whether you have adequate life insurance and disability coverages. If the worst happens—you must enter a nursing home—you might be able to qualify for financial assistance from the state by transferring your assets to a special needs trust for your son or daughter with a disability

Avoiding Guardianship and Conservatorship

Let's say that you suffer a disabling illness or injury that is serious enough to interfere with your day-to-day functioning. Your bills pile up because you cannot perform routine financial tasks such as making bank deposits, managing your investments, or just signing your name to checks. Let's also say that you need medical care, but you have become cognitively disabled and cannot understand the treatments your doctors are proposing. Any of these situations could require the appointment of a legal guardian or conservator to act on your behalf.[15]

As an attorney who has been involved in many probate court proceedings over the years, I recommend that you avoid court involvement if you can. The court process can be expensive, and all the fees are paid from your funds. The court process is not efficient either. Sometimes it can take several months for the court to appoint a guardian or conservator. However, you can avoid most if not all these costs and delays by proper advance planning.

Incapacity Documents

For most people, three routine, inexpensive documents are sufficient to avoid guardianship and conservatorship if they become seriously disabled. These documents are the durable power of attorney, health care proxy, and living will.

Durable power of attorney

A durable power of attorney (DPA) allows another person to take over managing your finances if you cannot do so yourself. In the Guardianship section, I explained how your son or daughter with a disability could appoint you to be his or her DPA agent. In some cases, this can avoid the necessity of guardianship.

For your own DPA, you can appoint your spouse or another person to be your agent. Like the DPA your son or daughter signs, this

---

15 A guardian makes decisions in the areas of medical care, living arrangements, etc. A conservator manages a person's finances.

document will allow your agent to perform routine financial tasks such as:

- Write checks to pay your bills
- Invest your money
- Sign your income tax returns
- Deal with medical insurance benefits
- Claim disability retirement benefits
- Make withdrawals from a retirement account
- Refinance your mortgage
- Borrow against your home

In addition to these routine financial tasks, you can also protect your family financially by authorizing your agent to:

- Run your business, including a partnership, until your health improves or your interest can be sold
- Use your funds to make gifts to your family members. It could be critical to reduce your funds if you need to qualify for Medicaid benefits or reduce estate taxes.
- Transfer your assets to an existing special needs trust for your son or daughter with a disability or establish that kind of trust
- Exercise the rights you reserved to yourself as the donor of your son's or daughter's special needs trust

To be valid, the DPA must be signed and notarized.

You need to decide when the DPA will take effect. In most cases, the DPA becomes operative as soon as you sign it. Then you and the agent can put the DPA away and hope it will never be needed. Even so, you might worry about the possibility of wrongdoing. After all, the agent could conceivably use the DPA to act to your detriment while you are still healthy and capable, or the DPA could fall into the wrong hands.

If this is a concern, you could sign a so-called *springing durable power of attorney* that does not come into effect unless and until you become disabled. To use that kind of DPA, the agent must show evidence (usually a doctor's affidavit) that you are incapacitated. There can be a potential downside to the "springing" DPA. Some banks and other financial institutions might be reluctant to accept your agent's proof that you are incapacitated without additional verification.

Health care proxy

A health care proxy, which is discussed in the Guardianship section, allows another person to make medical decisions for you if you are disabled and cannot act for yourself. The health care proxy is commonplace in hospitals these days, as anyone who has undergone a surgical procedure can probably attest. If you sign a health care proxy, make sure it includes the new HIPPA language. That way, the healthcare providers must abide by your wishes.

Living will

A living will allows you to tell your family, healthcare agent, and healthcare providers the specific treatments you would want (or not want) if you were unable to speak for yourself. For example, you can say that if you are terminally ill or permanently unconscious, you would not want any "heroic measures" or artificial life supports.

One caveat: a living will is not necessarily legally binding in Massachusetts. If a dispute should arise about your care, the court might have to step in. However, if that should occur, a living will could be evidence of your preferences when you were healthy and able to speak for yourself.

How Will You Get By Financially?

Many people who become disabled face financial hardships—reduced or even no income, mounting medical bills, and rapidly depleting assets. Money worries can be especially troubling if you have made a financial commitment to assist your son or daughter with a disability in the future.

You can take steps while you are healthy to help avert a future crisis. You can have a financial planner evaluate your insurance needs and recommend disability, long-term care, and/or life insurance coverage. If you should become disabled, public benefit programs can replace lost income and pay for medical care. And if a catastrophe should strike and you must go into a nursing home, you may be able to preserve your assets for your child with a disability by transferring them to a special needs "payback" trust.

Role of the financial planner

A financial planner can play a valuable role in helping you prepare for a potential disability. Is your medical insurance adequate? If you are not sure, a financial planner can review your policy and make recommendations. You might decide to change plans or purchase supplemental insurance, such as Medex, which is offered through Blue Cross and Blue Shield.

How would you replace lost income? A financial planner can review any existing employer-sponsored short- or long-term disability insurance plans. If your coverage is not adequate, you could consider purchasing supplemental coverage. If your employer does not offer any coverage, or if you are self-employed, you could obtain private disability insurance.

What if you might need long-term care in a nursing home? To avoid depleting your assets, you can obtain long-term care insurance to pay for nursing home costs. This kind of insurance, which is regulated by the state, provides home care benefits, which can help you avoid a nursing home. Another advantage is that most plans pay benefits for at least four years. This can buy valuable time for you to arrange your finances to qualify for state-funded care.

Last, the financial planner can calculate the amount of life insurance you need to protect your survivors. If your coverage falls short, you can purchase a term, universal, or whole life policy. Chapter 27 "Life Insurance," discusses life insurance coverage.

Public benefit programs that replace income

Parents sometimes wonder whether the same government programs that assist their children might help them if they become disabled. In fact, two programs—SSI and SSDI—pay a monthly stream of income to people with disabilities. These two programs are also discussed in the SSI section. (See Chapter 1, "Overview of SSI," and Chapter 10, "SSDI, Medicare, Medicaid, and Related Programs.")

Social Security Disability Insurance (SSDI) will pay you and your dependents a monthly cash benefit. To qualify, you must be under age 65, have made sufficient payments into the Social Security retirement system, and have been disabled for at least five months. The amount of benefits, which is subject to a family maximum, is tied to your earnings record. There is no asset limit for SSDI. You can keep your assets and still receive benefits.

Supplemental Security Income (SSI) will pay you income if you do not qualify for SSDI or if your monthly SSDI benefit is lower than the SSI benefit rate for your particular category. In Massachusetts, the SSI monthly benefit amounts range from $633 to $1,057 per month (in 2010 for a single person). There are strict asset limits for SSI. You may not retain more than $2,000 in countable resources. SSI does not pay any benefits to your dependents.

Public benefit programs that pay for medical expenses

After you have qualified for SSDI for 24 months, you can obtain Medicare insurance. Medicare pays for up to 35 hours per week of skilled care at home. (Skilled care involves procedures like intravenous injections, changing dressings, or physical therapy.) Medicare does not cover any custodial care such as help with bathing, dressing, going to the bathroom, or eating (although most private long-term care policies do cover that kind of care). Medicare also pays for up to 150 days of skilled care in a nursing home.

Public benefit programs that pay for prescription drugs

Medicare pays for a limited amount of prescription drugs. (See Chapter 10, "SSDI, Medicare, MassHealth, and Related Programs.") In Massachusetts, people age 65 and over and individuals with disabilities of any age can get help to pay for prescription drugs through the Prescription Advantage program. There may be an annual premium, which is set on a sliding scale according to income, as well as co-payments and deductibles.

Public benefit programs that pay for nursing home care

With the average cost of a nursing home stay in Massachusetts costing about $300 per day (over $100,000 per year), families are understandably concerned that a catastrophic illness could wipe out their savings. If you do not have any long-term care insurance and cannot afford to pay privately for your or your spouse's care, you may have to ask the state for help. In Massachusetts, that means obtaining Medicaid long-term care benefits.

To qualify for those benefits, you must exhaust your financial resources. If you are single, you can keep no more than $2,000 in assets. If you are married, the healthy spouse can keep the principal residence and up to about $109,000 in other resources (in 2010). To discourage you from giving away your assets to reach these limits, however, the state may impose a waiting period to get benefits. In general, the state "looks back" 60 months prior to the date you apply for benefits to see whether you have made any gifts or other uncompensated transfers. If you have transferred any property during the look-back period, there will be a waiting period to get benefits. The length of the waiting period depends on the amount of property you transferred.

Special Needs Trusts and Nursing Home Expenses

If you or your spouse are about to be admitted to a nursing home, you can transfer your assets directly to your son or daughter with a disability or to a trust for his or her benefit. Once the assets have been transferred, you or your spouse can qualify for Medicaid benefits right away. This is an exception to the 60-month waiting period described earlier.

This strategy isn't just for parents. Anyone, such as a grandparent or other relative, can give assets to a person with a disability and obtain nursing home benefits right away. To qualify, the disabled recipient of the property (or trust beneficiary) must be under age 65 and permanently and totally disabled. In this case, being "disabled" means that the person receives SSI or SSDI or meets the disability standards for those programs.

Do not transfer your assets to your estate planning special needs trust

Perhaps you, your parent, or another relative are considering transferring assets to a trust in order to qualify for nursing-home level Medicaid benefits. If so, you should probably not transfer the assets to a special needs trust that was prepared as part of an estate plan. The chances are, it won't have the necessary wording to satisfy the state Medicaid office. To qualify for nursing-home level Medicaid benefits, you will need a particular kind of special needs trust that is sometimes referred to as a "payback trust" or "D4A trust." (The federal law that authorizes this kind of trust is 42 U.S.C. 1396p(d)(4)(A).) The "payback" is the requirement that when the beneficiary dies, any funds that remain in the trust must be used to pay back the state for the beneficiary's Medicaid costs. This kind of trust must also meet other criteria. It must:

- Be irrevocable
- Be created by the beneficiary's parent, grandparent, or legal guardian, or by a court
- Benefit only the person with a disability. Other family members may not benefit, although these family members may be the remainder beneficiaries who will receive the trust proceeds when the beneficiary with a disability dies and the trust ends.
- Provide that when the beneficiary with a disability passes on, the state Medicaid agency will be the first payee; not even the beneficiary's funeral costs can have priority

When either you or your spouse intend to qualify for Medicaid benefits, neither of you can be the trustee. There must be an independent trustee who is not related to you.

Laying the groundwork

To take advantage of this last minute tactic, it helps to do some advance planning while you are still healthy. Your attorney can prepare a special needs trust that can be amended by the trustee. If you should need nursing home care and want the state to pay your expenses, the trustee can amend the trust to add the necessary "payback" language. Then you can transfer your excess funds to the trust and qualify immediately for nursing home level benefits under Medicaid. If you don't need those benefits, the trust would not need to be amended. The remaining funds in the trust can pass as you originally specified—to your family or favorite charities instead of the state.

A court can approve the transfer to a trust

What if you (or your son's or daughter's grandparent) failed to do any advance planning and are now too sick to take any action? Does that mean that nothing can be done? Not necessarily. In some cases, the family can ask the court to approve the transfer. However, the court process can be expensive, time consuming, and uncertain. Nevertheless, many families would agree that it is preferable to incur these costs and delays rather than spend their last dollars on nursing home care.

26

Beyond the Basics

Topics include

Revocable trust for minor children
Living trust
Bypass trust
Life insurance trust

For many families, a satisfactory estate plan will consist of wills, a special needs trust, and the incapacity documents discussed in the previous chapter. But perhaps you want to reduce estate taxes, avoid probate costs, or protect your children's inheritance from a former spouse or partner. In that case, you may need to go beyond the basics. This chapter explains strategies to do so.

An Unfunded Revocable Trust Can Protect Minor Children

As I explained earlier, a minor child under age 18 who inherits any property, life insurance, or retirement assets can get control of those assets at age 18. Most parents think this is much too young to receive a substantial inheritance. To prevent your child from getting access to an inheritance at this young age, you can include a *testamentary trust* in your will. (See Chapter 22, "Using a Will to Plan Your Estate.") This kind of trust grants management of your child's inheritance to a trustee to hold until the child reaches an age that you say is appropriate, perhaps 25 or 28. These trusts can have drawbacks, such as steep court costs and uncertainty about who will be in charge.

An improvement over the testamentary trust is an *unfunded*

revocable trust. This kind of trust is separate from your will. The term "unfunded" means that the trust does not contain any assets while you are still alive. Property does not flow into the trust until after your death. Unlike a testamentary trust, court involvement is minimal, so your survivors' administrative costs are less. You also have the security of knowing that the people you nominate as trustees will be in charge. This can be welcome news for single and divorced parents.

Administrative costs are reduced

An unfunded revocable trust is usually less expensive to manage than a testamentary trust. This is because there is little if any court oversight. With a testamentary trust, the trustee must file detailed annual financial accounts with the probate court that show what has been done with the child's money. Then a guardian *ad litem* (GAL) will be appointed to look over the accounts on the child's behalf. The fees for preparing, filing, and reviewing the accounts are all paid from the child's funds.

In contrast, with a revocable trust, you can decide the accounting requirements when you set up the trust. For example, you can say that the trustee will provide the account directly to your son or daughter (or his or her legal guardian, if there is one) or to another family member. But the bottom line is that avoiding court oversight almost always saves money.

The trustees you select will be in charge

Another potential disadvantage to the testamentary trust is that the probate court judge could override your choice of trustee and appoint a "neutral" person to serve. This occurred recently in a probate court case proceeding. A grandmother had set up a testamentary trust for her grandson and named another relative to be the trustee. But the grandson's mother complained to the Court about the relative. The result was that someone the family had never met was put in charge of the grandson's trust. For the next 15 years, that person will handle the money and make important spending decisions.

Who will manage your son's or daughter's inheritance could be a special concern if you are a single or divorced parent. If that is the case, you should not use a testamentary trust, because your former spouse or partner could persuade the judge that he or she—not the person you have chosen—should be the trustee. However, you don't run that risk with a private trust arrangement. Since there is minimal court involvement, your ex probably could not interfere with your plans. That means that the people you select when you set up the trust—perhaps a parent or sibling—will be in charge.

A Living Trust Can Reduce Probate Costs

Depending on your personal circumstances, a living trust may be a useful estate planning tool. Unlike a will, which takes effect on your death, a living trust becomes operational while you are alive. A living trust is sometimes called an *inter vivos* trust. The way it works is fairly straightforward. Instead of owning assets in your own name, you re-title your assets in the name of your revocable living trust. As the "grantor" and initial trustee of the trust, you retain full control of your assets while you are alive and healthy. The trust is fully revocable so that you can change its terms or even cancel it altogether. If you become disabled or die, the successor trustee that you have named can take over managing the assets.

Advantages of a living trust

A living trust lets you avoid the probate process. Probate proceedings are not needed because the living trust already owns the property. When you are gone, the successor trustee simply dissolves the trust and distributes the property to the individuals you have designated to receive it. Alternatively, the trustee can continue to manage the trust for one or more beneficiaries, such as your son or daughter with a disability.

A revocable living trust can be especially useful if you own real estate in more than one state. In most states, when a property owner dies, the heirs must bring probate proceedings in that state in order to clear title. However, if a trust owns the real estate, probate is not needed because the trust—not the deceased individual—holds legal title.

Another advantage is that if you suffer a disabling illness, your successor trustee can step in to manage your property. The trustee can pay your bills, invest your funds, deal with your retirement plan, and pay your taxes. Of course, you can achieve a similar result by appointing someone as your agent under a durable power of attorney (discussed in Chapter 25, "Planning for Your Own Incapacity"). However, some advisors believe that a living trust can cover more contingencies and is less likely to be challenged. Since the assets are already owned by the trust, ownership can pass seamlessly to the successor trustee.

Limitations of a living trust

A living trust has some limitations and downsides:

- You lose protections from creditors that are available for your principal residence. In Massachusetts, a person can protect the equity in his or her residence by declaring a homestead. Currently, an individual can protect up to $500,000, and a couple age 65 or older can get even more protection. Married couples can obtain similar protections by owning their residence as tenants by the entirety. That kind of ownership will protect a principal residence occupied by both spouses. (Both homestead and tenancy by the entirety are discussed in Chapter 28, "Money Matters.") These two important protections cannot be used if the residence is owned through a living trust.
- You will not save any estate taxes by using a living trust. Your estate tax liability will be the same whether you have a will or a living trust. Any assets owned by the living trust are subject to federal and Massachusetts estate taxes, the same as if they were titled in your own name.
- For a living trust to be effective, you must diligently follow through and re-title all your assets in the name of the trust. These assets include your residence, checking and savings accounts, investments, and automobiles. If you omit any assets, they could be subject to probate, which would defeat the purpose of your living trust.

Where to learn more

It is relatively easy to find an attorney to set up a living trust. You can go to one of the free introductory seminars that are offered in your area. But before you go, be sure to read up on the subject so you will know what questions to ask. Your public library probably has several comprehensive books on the subject. To find out about the downside of living trusts, I recommend law professor John Huggard's book *Living Trust, Living Hell* (listed in the Resources section).

A Bypass Trust Can Reduce Estate Taxes

Estate taxes—both federal and Massachusetts—could reduce the amount of property your survivors receive. Fortunately, not everyone has to be concerned about estate taxes. For one thing, you can leave any amount of money to your spouse free of estate taxes, provided that he or she is a U.S. citizen. This is called *the unlimited marital deduction.* If your spouse is not a U.S. citizen, you can use a special kind of trust called a Marital Qualified Domestic Trust (QDOT) to reduce or eliminate the estate tax.

In 2009, if you were not married or if you wanted to leave property to someone other than your spouse (such as your children), you could leave up to $3.5 million without paying any federal estate tax. The amount you can leave free of estate taxes is called the *personal exemption.* Due to a wrinkle in the law, there is no estate tax in 2010. In 2011, the personal exemption amount will be $1 million. However, most analysts expect Congress to change the law by making the personal exemption about $3.5 million per person. This could be retroactive to January 2010.

Massachusetts also has an unlimited marital deduction. However, the personal exemption is only $1 million (in 2010). This exemption amount is expected to remain constant for the indefinite future.

Let's say that you are married and your family's net worth (including all life insurance policies) is $1.5 million. You don't need to worry about estate taxes, right? Not necessarily. It's true that you can leave everything to your spouse free of estate taxes. But when your spouses passes on, the inherited property—together with your spouse's own separate assets—could easily amount to $1.5 million or more, putting his or her estate within reach of the Massachusetts estate tax. You might want to consider some strategies to reduce estate taxes that are discussed in this section. However, if your family's net worth is $1 million or less, you probably do not need to take any special steps to reduce estate taxes, because none would be owed.

What is included in your taxable estate?

Your taxable estate will include everything you own when you die. That could include items like your personal residence; retirement accounts like IRAs and 401(k)s; investments (stocks, bonds, and mutual funds); life insurance policies; and personal property such as automobiles, jewelry, and works of art.

How much is the estate tax?

At the end of 2009, the federal tax rate began at 18% for amounts over $3.5 million. If and when Congress passes a new estate tax law, the rates will probably be different. Massachusetts taxes any assets over $1 million on a sliding scale up to 15%.

How a bypass trust operates

The purpose of a *bypass trust* (also called a *credit shelter trust* or *family trust)* is to preserve each person's personal exemption and also take advantage of the unlimited marital deduction. Let me give you an example. Let's say that a married couple owns $2 million of assets. Each spouse establishes a revocable living trust and funds it with assets worth up to the personal exemption amount, which is $1 million in Massachusetts.

When the first spouses dies—let's say it is the husband—his revocable trust will automatically create two new trusts: a *credit shelter trust* for the children (and, if desired, for the wife as well) and a *marital trust* solely for the wife. Up to $1 million could go into the credit shelter trust. No estate tax would be due, because the contribution is covered by the personal exemption amount. The funds in the credit shelter trust would not be distributed to the children right away. Instead, as long as the wife is alive, she can get the income and some of the principal from the trust. Any of the husband's assets over $1 million could pass to the wife, either outright or through the marital trust. Because of the unlimited marital deduction, this money would not trigger an estate tax.

When the wife dies, the funds in the credit shelter trust would be distributed to the children. No estate tax would be due, even if the principal has doubled in value, because the trust property has "by-passed" the wife's estate. Also, the wife's own property would qualify for the $1 million personal exemption. This allows the couple to pass $2 million to their children without paying any Massachusetts estate tax.

To be effective, a bypass trust requires some advance planning. For one thing, you and your spouse may have to divide and re-title your assets. The goal is to have each spouse own roughly the same amount of assets. If you both own all your assets jointly, the trust will not work; because the assets will pass directly to your spouse—not the trust. The trust terms must be somewhat restrictive. In order for your estate to get the maximum benefits, the credit shelter trust should have an independent trustee (someone who is not related by blood to your surviving spouse). Typically, the spouse and a relative of the deceased spouse will be co-trustees. If you do not want to have an independent trustee, your spouse's right to withdraw principal from the trust should be limited. For example, he or she might be permitted to withdraw only $5,000 or 5% of the principal in any year.

An Irrevocable Life Insurance Trust Can Reduce Estate Taxes

If estate taxes are a concern, you could buy life insurance to pay the taxes. But life insurance proceeds can add value to your estate, so the more insurance you own, the larger the estate tax. You can avoid this problem by owning life insurance through an *irrevocable life insurance trust* (ILIT).

An ILIT is a trust that is both the owner and beneficiary of a life insurance policy. To pay the premiums, you give money directly to the trustee. An ILIT can be rather restrictive:

- There must be an independent trustee. Under the IRS rules, the trustee cannot be, among others, the grantor (creator) of the trust or the grantor's spouse, parent, sibling, child, or grandchild.
- The trust must be irrevocable. That means that once you set up the trust, you cannot change the terms, including the beneficiaries.
- You cannot borrow against the life insurance policy or have any access to its cash value.

If you can live with these restrictions, an ILIT can be an effective way to own life insurance. Since the ILIT is a separate trust with an independent trustee, the policy is protected from your creditors. Creditors can include a nursing home, if you should need long-term care.

An ILIT can also be used as a special needs trust for a son or daughter with a disability. A popular way to fund an ILIT is with second-to-die life insurance (discussed in the next chapter). When the surviving spouse dies, the trustee can either distribute the life insurance proceeds to a special needs trust or continue to manage the ILIT for the beneficiary with a disability.

Timing is important for setting up an ILIT. If you fund the trust with an existing life insurance policy in which you have an ownership interest, you must set up the trust at least three years before your death. Otherwise, your estate will be taxed on the proceeds. However, if your trustee purchases a new policy more than three years before your death, your estate would not be taxed.

A Family Limited Partnership Can Reduce Estate Taxes

Some wealthy families (with assets in the $3 million to $5 million range) can benefit from establishing a family limited partnership. This technique can be especially useful if there are any valuable assets such as investment real estate or a family business. In this rather complicated arrangement, the parents and children create a partnership in which the parents are the general partners and the children are limited partners. The parents gradually transfer interests in the partnership to the children. Since the children are not in control, the value of their interests is heavily discounted from the item's fair market value.

It should be noted that the Internal Revenue Service often audits these arrangements. If the partners have not been careful to properly organize and scrupulously manage the business, the arrangement may be disallowed. However, if the partners are careful to observe the formalities, the desired results can be achieved. The parents can transfer substantial assets to the children without incurring any estate or gift taxes.

27

Life Insurance

Topics include

How much life insurance do you need?
Temporary life insurance
Permanent life insurance

Life insurance can be an important part of an estate plan. Most likely, you want to make certain that, on your death, your survivors will have adequate funds. Life insurance can create an instant estate to support and educate your children. Life insurance can also guarantee that there will be money to pass on to a child with a disability. But deciding how much insurance to buy—and what kind—can be complicated. This chapter covers the different kinds of life insurance and how to decide the amount you will need.

How Much Life Insurance Do You Need?

The first step in buying life insurance is to figure out how much protection you need. You will need to plan for your spouse, your special needs child, and your children without disabilities. The general idea is to help your family maintain their current lifestyle if your income is lost. For your child with a disability, you will need to anticipate the future cost of support.

There is no magic formula to come up with the right amount of insurance. This is a uniquely personal decision that will be based on several factors, including your current income, your family's standard of living, and projected future expenses.

Another factor to consider is the cost of life insurance. After all, it makes no sense to deprive your family now to pay for excessive amounts of life insurance they might not need later.

When it comes to planning for your spouse and children without disabilities, a lot of information is available on the Internet. Most of the large insurance companies, such as MetLife, John Hancock, and Prudential Insurance, offer online calculators to help you assess your life insurance needs. Some of the calculators are relatively simple, and some are quite elaborate. They all use a similar formula that involves calculating your survivors' future expenses and offsetting those against available resources, such as pension benefits, Social Security Survivors benefits, and lump sum death benefits. Your insurance agent probably has his or her own method for calculating your needs.

What are the Different Kinds of Life Insurance?

There are two basic kinds of life insurance: term insurance and permanent insurance. Term insurance is sometimes called "temporary" insurance because it expires at the end of a specific term. Permanent insurance is intended to last for your entire life. Depending on your circumstances, either kind of insurance policy can meet your needs at any particular time, and it might even be appropriate to have both kinds of insurance at the same time.

Term insurance. When you buy term insurance, you get protection only for a specific period of time. The term can last anywhere from one year to 15 or even 20 years. If you die during the term, the company will pay the face amount of the policy ("death benefit") to the people you have named as beneficiaries. Most term policies offer only a death benefit, with no savings component. There is no "cash value."

- Cost: The cost of term insurance is almost always lower than permanent insurance. If you are young, the premiums for term insurance can be relatively inexpensive, because your chances of dying are low. However, as you age, the premiums rise, because your risk of dying is greater. When you reach your 60s or 70s, the cost can become prohibitive.

- Renewability: You may not be able to renew term insurance if your health declines. However, some term policies will guarantee in advance that your policy can be renewed for another term, without any proof that you are still insurable. Some term policies can be converted to permanent insurance, such as whole life. Usually you must pay extra for this feature.
- Convenience: A benefit of cash value insurance is that you can buy only as much coverage as you need at any given time. When you don't need the coverage any more—like when your youngest child finishes school—you can cancel the coverage.

Permanent insurance. Unlike term insurance, permanent (also called cash value) insurance is designed to last your whole life. It combines term insurance with a savings component. There are three basic kinds of permanent insurance: whole life, universal life, and variable life (see the box later in this chapter). A joint life policy (discussed below) can insure two lives.

- Cost: Permanent insurance almost always costs more than term insurance. Unlike term insurance, where you are paying only for death protection, your premium for permanent insurance buys both life insurance protection and a cash fund. In the early years of the policy, the portion of the premium that is not used for insurance protection is applied to the policy's cash value. In the later years of the policy, the cash value can be used to pay the premiums.
- Renewability: A benefit of whole life insurance is that you don't need to remain healthy to renew your coverage from year to year. As long as you pay the premiums, your policy cannot be cancelled.
- Flexibility: Permanent insurance can be more flexible than term insurance because the premiums are not necessarily fixed. For example, with universal and variable life policies, you can select what the company calls a "target premium." This target premium is designed to keep the policy in effect for your whole life. Within limits, you can reduce or even temporarily stop paying the annual premium. During that time, the money in the cash fund can be used to pay the premium. Of course, if

there is not enough money in the cash fund to pay the premium in any particular year, you must come up with the money or your coverage will be cancelled.

- Investment: If you cancel a permanent policy, you may be able to get some of your premiums back. This is not the case with a term policy.

- Tax benefits: There are tax benefits available with a permanent policy that are not available with term insurance or even ordinary investments. For example, let's say that you invest in an ordinary mutual fund that earns interest and dividends. The income is taxed in the year it is earned. By contrast, any earnings on a cash value policy are not taxed until they are actually withdrawn. And even then, you won't necessarily have to pay tax on all the earnings. Let's say that you have a $250,000 policy for which you have paid $8,000 in premiums to keep your life insured and have also built up $10,000 in cash value. If you withdraw the entire $10,000, you would only pay income tax on $2,000. You can deduct the cost of the life insurance protection. Another tax advantage is that your beneficiaries do not have to pay any income tax when you die. They can receive the entire policy income tax free. However, your estate might have to pay estate taxes on the policy, depending on how many other assets you own when you die.

Joint life insurance. Joint life insurance is a special kind of permanent insurance. As the name suggests, a joint policy covers two lives, usually a husband and wife. There are two kinds of joint life insurance: first-to-die insurance and second-to-die insurance. With a first-to-die policy, benefits are paid when the first spouse dies. The beneficiary is usually the surviving spouse. With a second-to-die policy, no benefits are paid until the second spouse dies. The beneficiaries are usually the surviving children, a special needs trust, or both. Joint life policies are popular because the premiums are usually lower than two separate cash value policies. However, second-to-die coverage is probably not appropriate for younger couples. After all, if your spouse died unexpectedly in his or her 30s or 40s, would you want to wait 40 or even 50 years for your survivors to receive payment?

Kinds of Permanent Insurance

Whole life: This is the most basic kind of permanent life insurance you can buy. The premiums and death benefit stay constant from year to year, and there is a guaranteed cash value.

Universal life: The premiums and death benefit can vary from year to year. Some of the premiums go into a savings fund. Unlike whole life, the return on the savings fund is not guaranteed.

Variable life: This is the riskiest kind of insurance. It is up to you to invest the cash value portion of the policy in stocks, bonds, and money funds. Both the amount of the death benefit and the cash value of the policy will depend on your skills as an investor.

Consider an insurance company's financial strength

In addition to the kind of life insurance you buy, you should also consider the financial stability of a particular insurance company. If the company becomes insolvent, you could lose your coverage and have nothing to show for your premiums. Before buying a policy, look up the company's rating in *Best's Insurance Reports*, which can be found in most public libraries or online at http://www.ambest.com. The ratings go from A++ to F. Most advisors recommend that you buy life insurance from a company that is rated at least A.

Life Insurance and the Child with Special Needs

Parents are often advised to maintain life insurance as a way to make sure that their son or daughter with a disability will have some funds after they are gone. This is sound advice. Before you purchase a policy, however, you must decide how much coverage you need and what kind of policy is best.

How much life insurance should you carry?

Figuring out how much life insurance you should carry can be difficult. A traditional life insurance analysis would focus on the future financial need and the available resources. But this analysis does not always work for a child with a disability. The actual numbers can be hard to nail down because the cost of future care is uncertain. You would need to factor in the availability of public benefits to pay for your son's or daughter's care. Predicting in advance what these resources will amount to is difficult. As a result, many families end up buying coverage—anywhere from $100,000 to $500,000—based on what they can afford to pay. That may not be the most mathematically precise way to go about buying life insurance, but it makes sense. These families have made sure that a substantial asset will be available, and if their son's or daughter's needs change, the coverage can be adjusted.

What kind of life insurance is best?

As the parent of a child with a disability, you will probably want to keep the life insurance coverage in effect for your entire life. Term insurance is not usually recommended because the cost becomes prohibitive as you age. Another disadvantage of term insurance is that you may not be able to renew your coverage if your health declines. Your coverage could end when you are sick and need it most.

If you want to guarantee that there will be continuous coverage, permanent insurance is preferable. When you initially take out the policy, the premiums are set with the goal that you will maintain the policy for your entire life. Typically, the payment schedule can be structured so that you will finish paying premiums by the time you retire. Your premiums will end when your income declines. Another plus is the comfort factor. If the permanent insurance is already paid up, you will not have to worry that every dollar you spend in retirement will take money away from your son or daughter with a disability.

Life Insurance Trusts

A dependable way to own permanent life insurance is through a special needs trust or an irrevocable life insurance trust (ILIT) that has been created specifically for that purpose. Since an independent entity (the trust) owns the policy, the proceeds are not part of your estate. This means the proceeds of the policy are not subject to estate tax on your death. Also, the policy's cash value is protected from your creditors, including nursing homes if either you or your spouse should need long-term care. Chapter 26, "Beyond the Basics," discusses life insurance trusts.

28

Money Matters

Topics include

Financial planners
Declaration of homestead
Saving for a child with a disability
A state sponsored retirement savings plan

This chapter focuses on the financial aspects of estate planning. After all, one way to protect your family after you are gone is to make the most of the assets you have while you are here. A financial planner can help you do that through sound investing, retirement planning, and prudent saving.

You should also think about protecting what you own. I cover two easy strategies to protect the equity in your home from your creditors. When it comes to saving money for a child with a disability, parents often ask, "What is the best way to save money—through a special needs trust, or some other way?" This chapter explains the various choices.

Since many families start the estate planning process by hiring a financial planner, I begin with that topic—what financial planners do, what they cost, and how to find a qualified one.

Working with a Financial Planner

A good financial planner can provide a broad range of services. He or she can help you identify your goals and develop a plan to achieve them. The person can also help you analyze financial products such as life insurance policies, long-term care insurance, and annuities. If any estate planning or tax issues come up, he or she can refer you to a qualified tax professional or attorney. Last, a financial planner can also function as an investment advisor by recommending specific investments. Some can even take over managing your savings.

The planning process

A financial planner typically begins by taking an inventory of what you currently have. What are your assets and how are they owned? Do you have any life insurance and retirement savings? How much money do you and your spouse earn? What are your expenses and debts?

Next, you begin the process of clarifying your goals. Perhaps you want to send your children without disabilities to college and also save money for your special needs child. Perhaps one parent wants to leave work temporarily to stay home with young children. You might want to purchase a larger home or a vacation home. And you might wonder whether you can ever afford to retire.

A financial planner can help you assess whether you can achieve your goals. If you find your goals are not realistic, you will need to scale back or prioritize them. Once you have established goals, your financial planner can help you develop a strategy to achieve them. That strategy could involve making more productive use of your assets through prudent investing or debt reduction.

You don't want to see your plans disrupted by any unforeseen events, such as your disability or premature death, an accident, or a lawsuit. Thus, you should have sufficient insurance in place, including life, health, accident, and disability coverage. Your financial planner can review your current coverages and determine if they are adequate. If you need more insurance, he or she can help you purchase the appropriate products.

A solid financial plan also includes an estate planning component. You should have a plan to provide for your survivors in the event of your premature death. Toward this end, typically a financial planner and attorney will work together. Your attorney can make sure that the necessary documents, such as wills and trusts, are in place. He or she should also provide you with the correct wording for the beneficiary designations on your life insurance policies and retirement accounts.

Last, a financial planner should heed your tolerance for risk. If you cannot stand the thought of your investments losing money, your financial planner should take this into account. After all, an overly aggressive investment strategy will not do you much good if it keeps you awake at night.

Qualifications, compensation, and cost

Where can you find a qualified financial planner? Often a good referral source is other families who have worked with a particular person. Sometimes the Arcs and similar organizations sponsor workshops on this topic, which can give you a chance to meet a financial planner. Your attorney may also be able to put you in touch with a qualified person. The Resources section of this book also includes some suggestions.

You will want to make sure that the financial planner you are considering is qualified to do the job and is trustworthy. The issue of qualifications can be problematic. Almost anyone can use the designation "financial planner," and individuals who hold themselves out as such often have a bewildering array of letters after their names.

If the person's qualifications are important to you, then you should hire a certified financial planner. These individuals are licensed by the Certified Financial Planner Board of Standards, which sets high standards for its members. To obtain the CFP designation, a person must have at least three years experience in the field and pass a comprehensive exam. A CFP must take continuing education courses. This can assure that they will stay on top of new developments. If you have a complaint, you can register it with the Board of Standards, which will investigate. Last, you can find out if a particular financial planner has had any complaints lodged against him or her by going to the Board's website, http://www.cfp.net.

After you have obtained some names of financial planners, plan to meet with two or three of them. Most individuals will not charge anything for a brief "get acquainted" meeting. At the meeting, you can ask key questions about their background, fees, and method of payment (commission, fee based, or both—see below). You should also ask about their experience working with families who have a child with a disability.

In general, there are two different method of compensation: commissions and fees. Before you hire the planner, be clear about how he or she will be paid. It is usually best to go with a "fee-only" financial planner. They usually charge one flat rate for a complete financial plan. However, there are exceptions. For example, some fee-only financial planners will charge an hourly rate if they only work on one specific task, such as reviewing a particular annuity or insurance policy. If you just want to purchase life insurance, you might not have to pay anything except the annual premium. The financial planner's compensation—typically a percentage of the first year's premium—will be paid directly by the insurance company.

By contrast, some financial planners only work on a commission basis. These individuals are paid from the commissions they receive from the investments you purchase as a result of their advice. Sometimes this can set up a potential conflict of interest. You cannot be certain whether the financial planner has recommended a particular investment because it is best for you, or because it will generate a large commission.

How much should you expect to pay for financial planning services? In eastern Massachusetts, you should plan to pay about $1,200 to $1,500 for a comprehensive financial plan (in 2010). The costs may be slightly lower in the central and western parts of the state.

Protecting Your Home

Like many people, your home may be your most valuable asset. Your home probably figures prominently in your plans to pass along money to your children, including your child with a disability. You want to ensure that you do not lose your home (or its equity) because of unmanageable personal or business debt.

In Massachusetts, two inexpensive methods can protect your principal residence—the homestead declaration and tenancy by the entirety. Within limits, both will protect the equity in your home in case of certain unpaid debts. The homestead and tenancy by entirety are not mutually exclusive. You can use them together to prevent a forced sale of your home.

Homestead declaration

Massachusetts allows a homeowner to declare a homestead of

$500,000 on his or her personal residence. For couples age 62 or older, the protection is even greater.

A homestead declaration is intended to prevent a creditor from forcing a sale of your home. For example, let's say your property is worth $500,000, and there is a $250,000 mortgage. Your $250,000 equity would be fully protected because it is less than the homestead amount. This means that if your house had to be sold to pay your debts, you could keep $250,000.

However, a homestead declaration does not necessarily afford complete protection if the equity in your home exceeds the homestead amount. For example, let's say that your home is worth $850,000 with a $250,000 mortgage. You have $600,000 in equity. A creditor could force a sale of your home and potentially collect $100,000 (the amount by which your $600,000 equity exceeds the $500,000 homestead amount).

A homestead declaration has some limitations. It will not protect you from any debts incurred before you filed for the homestead. And the homestead does not apply to mortgage debt, real estate taxes, income taxes, court ordered child support, or alimony. All those obligations would have to be paid before the homestead protection applies.

To claim homestead protection, you need to request it through a relatively easy process. You complete a Declaration of Homestead form and file it with the Registry of Deeds for the county where your property is located. The form can be obtained at any county Registry of Deeds office or online. (The Resources section contains a list of registries, listed by county.) There is a $35 filing fee. If you want an attorney to prepare and record the homestead, plan to pay about $50 to $75, plus the filing fee. If you re-finance your mortgage, your lender will probably require you to release the homestead. After the new loan has been recorded, however, you can re-file the homestead.

Last, to claim homestead protection, you must own your home in your own name. If you own your property through a trust, you cannot take advantage of homestead protection. Chapter 26, "Beyond the Basics," explains this.

Tenancy by the entirety

Tenancy by the entirety is a special kind of joint ownership that is only available to married couples. If a couple owns their principal residence as tenants by the entirety, a creditor cannot force a sale of the residence. In order to get the statutory protections, both spouses must occupy the residence.

In some cases, a tenancy by the entirety could offer more protection than a homestead declaration. With a homestead, a creditor can potentially force a sale of the property and collect any excess equity over the homestead exemption. With a tenancy by the entirety, no forced sale can take place as long as both spouses occupy the property. A creditor's only remedy is to file an attachment against the property and wait for some future event to occur that will end the tenancy, such as a divorce or sale of the property. If the spouse who owes the debt dies first, the attachment will end. This is because the surviving spouse will own the property free of the deceased spouse's debt.

A tenancy by the entirety does not offer complete protection. As noted, the death of a spouse will sever the tenancy. If the non-debtor spouse dies, the protection ends, and the creditors of the surviving debtor spouse may be able to force a sale. Also, there is no protection against debts that both spouses acquired jointly, such as a mortgage loan. There is no protection if the debt was acquired for "necessities" that were purchased for the family, such as medical care.

Money and the Child with a Disability

Many parents ask, "What is the best way to save money for my child with a disability?" Sometimes children receive small amounts of cash on birthdays, holidays, and other special occasions. Some grandparents hint that they intend to make a more substantial gift. Some children receive financial compensation as the result of an injury. And some parents want to save money for their child with a disability the same way they set up college funds for their other children. What is the best way to save this money until the child needs it? In general, the answer will depend on the amount of money involved and whether you are saving your child's money or your own money. Here are some options to consider.

Saving a child's money

When you are saving your child's money, you must be careful not to do anything that will impede the ability to get SSI at age 18. Unless the money will be held in an irrevocable trust (see below), you should not accumulate more than $2,000.

- **Direct registration and joint account.** For a very small amount of money (say, $500 or less), you could open a bank account in your son's or daughter's own name. A better idea, though, is to establish a joint account between you and your son or daughter. That way, you can make any additions or withdrawals on his or her behalf.
- **UTMA account.** Another way to save a small amount of money is through a Uniform Transfers to Minors Act (UTMA) bank account. (Chapter 2, "Qualifying for SSI," covers UTMA accounts.) As the UTMA custodian, you can hold the funds and make investment and spending decisions until your son or daughter reaches age 21. Unlike other kinds of assets that become countable when an SSI recipient reaches age 18, Social Security does not count most UTMA accounts until the recipient is age 21. Thus, there is a three-year grace period to reduce the money.
- **Irrevocable trust.** If there is a large amount of money, such as from the settlement of a lawsuit, these funds should be placed in an irrevocable special needs trust. Otherwise, the child cannot get SSI at age 18. The trust document must state that when the beneficiary dies, any remaining funds will be used to pay back the state for his or her Medicaid benefits. Chapter 3, "Reducing Assets to Qualify for SSI," discusses these so-called payback trusts.

Gifts from grandparents

Some grandparents have plans to make a *future gift* to their grandchildren under their wills. They should leave a grandchild's inheritance to a trust. The trust could be a special needs trust or some other kind of trust, as long as the grandchild does not have any control over the funds. The grandparent will need special language in his or her will or trust to direct the gift to the grandchild's trust. The correct language will assure that the funds will be properly managed and that the child can receive SSI at age 18.

Some wealthy grandparents may want to make a *present gift* to a grandchild. These grandparents are often motivated to avoid federal and state estate taxes that are imposed on large estates. Within certain limits, they can do so by giving away money. (See the box titled, "What is the gift tax?") If a grandchild with a disability will be the recipient of a substantial gift, the funds should be given to a trust for the child.

From the grandparents' perspective, there can be a complication with this approach. In order for the gift to meet the grandparents' tax planning needs, the grandchild's trust must have certain technical provisions. These withdrawal rights (*"Crummey powers"*) allow the grandchild to remove some of the trust funds each year in which a contribution is made. But most special needs trusts do not contain these provisions. Attorneys do not routinely include them for public benefits reasons. Having the right to withdraw funds can interfere with a child's ability to receive SSI at age 18. This is true even if the child never actually withdraws the funds.

In summary, a grandparent who wants to make a present gift to a grandchild with a disability and achieve tax savings faces a complicated situation. For grandparents to set up an appropriate arrangement, the parent's attorney and the grandparent's attorney must work together to develop a plan that will meet everyone's needs.

Parents saving their own money

Often parents want to save some of their money for a son or daughter with a disability. It is better to accumulate money in the parent's own name or save through a trust? When it comes to savings, there is no "one size fits all" approach. You need to do what makes sense in your particular situation. Most people prefer a simple arrangement that won't increase tax preparation fees or cause higher income taxes. Other people think reducing estate taxes or obtaining protection from creditors is important. Fortunately, whatever method you choose, you won't have to worry about SSI's strict $2,000 resource limit. Social Security disregards your personal savings as long as your son or daughter does not have any direct access to the money and you—and not your son or daughter—can control how the money will be used. Here are some ways to save some of your own money for your son or daughter with a disability.

- **Saving in your own name.** The least complicated arrangement is to set up a bank account or mutual fund in your own name. You could register the account as a "pay on death" (POD) account. That way, when you die, the funds can pass directly to your child's special needs trust. Tax reporting is simple because you use your own Social Security Number on the account and report any earnings on your personal income tax return. Are there any drawbacks to this approach? For some people, creditors are a concern. The savings account (like most other assets you own in your own name) would be accessible to your creditors if you were sued. And if you apply for college financial aid for your non-disabled son or daughter, the savings would be counted toward the family share that must be used before any aid would be granted. Also, when you die, your estate might owe estate taxes on the funds. That could reduce the amount you can leave estate tax free to your special needs son or daughter. Last, unless you are a disciplined saver, you might be tempted to withdraw the funds to spend on a new car, vacation, or tuition for your non-disabled son or daughter.
- **529 college savings plan.** If you believe your child with special needs might go on to post-secondary education, you can put money into a 529 college savings plan. The funds grow income-tax free while in the account, and they are not taxed on removal if they are spent on higher education. As long as you contribute your own money, these plans are not counted toward the $2,000 asset limit for SSI. If your son or daughter does not use the funds, you can name another beneficiary to receive them. However, the funds must be spent before the beneficiary's 25th birthday.
- **Revocable trust.** Another option is to use the revocable special needs trust that that your lawyer prepared with your estate planning documents. However, it is important to check with your attorney before you transfer any money to the trust to ensure

no unforeseen problems arise from using the trust this way. In general, saving money in a revocable trust is not much different from saving money in your own name. You use your own Social Security Number on the trust bank account and report the income on your personal income tax return. In Massachusetts, you are considered to personally own any funds you hold in a revocable trust. The trust funds are available to your creditors, counted for financial aid purposes, and included in your taxable estate. Despite these limitations, however, there may be one advantage: the guilt factor. Most of us would hesitate to dip into our child's trust fund to pay for our personal expenses, even if we originally contributed the money.

- **Irrevocable trust.** For most people, the costs of saving through an irrevocable trust will probably outweigh any potential benefits. Some of the disadvantages are:

> You would need an irrevocable trust document. The special needs trust your lawyer prepared with your estate plan is probably fully revocable. A revocable trust is an acceptable way to leave money to your child with a disability when you die. But it is not a very effective means to save money for you son or daughter while you are alive. Thus, you will need to pay a lawyer to amend your existing special needs trust or create a new one. Plan to spend anywhere from $1,200 to $2,500 for legal services (in 2010).

> You will also need to spend more money for tax preparation fees. An irrevocable trust is a separate taxpayer that must file its own income tax return every year. (Under IRS rules, the trust will need its own Employer Identification Number, which the IRS will assign. You can't use your own Social Security Number or your son's or daughter's Social Security Number.) Plan to pay about $250 for a basic return, more if the trust has spent any of its earnings.

You might pay more income taxes with an irrevocable trust. If the trust distributes any of its income, that income can be "passed through" to the beneficiary and reported on his or her personal income tax return. However, any income that the trust does not distribute or spend on administrative fees like tax preparation is taxed to the trust. The tax rates for trusts are higher than those for individuals. For example, in 2009, an individual did not reach the 35% maximum tax rate until he or she had $372,950 of taxable income. However, a trust reached the 35% maximum tax rate with only $11,150 of taxable income.[16]

What is the gift tax?

The federal gift tax applies to gifts over $13,000 per year (in 2010). You can give up to $13,000 per year to as many people as you wish without paying any gift tax. (A couple can give $26,000.) You can also pay unlimited amounts for another person's educational and medical expenses as long as you give the money directly to the institution or medical provider. Any gifts over $13,000 will reduce your lifetime gift limit, which is currently $1 million. This means that even if you give $20,000 to one person, you can still give away another $993,000 before any tax would be imposed. ($13,000 qualifies for the gift tax exclusion, leaving $7,000 that is applied to your lifetime limit.)

---

16 These figures are for the 2009 tax year. The tax rates for 2010 have not been set at the time this book is printed.

A State Sponsored Savings Plan May Be Coming to Massachusetts

Help for parents and others who want to save money for a child with a disability may be coming from the Commonwealth of Massachusetts. Reportedly, the state is considering implementing a "qualified savings plan" for children with disabilities. This would function like the state-approved U Plan for college investing. Funds could be set aside for a child's future needs. Those funds would grow income tax free. When they are withdrawn, no tax would be owed, as long as the funds are used for goods and services the person needs. Some examples of permitted expenses would be a residence (or share of one), furnishings, special therapies, equipment, and one-to-one assistance.

Part IV: Loose Ends

29

Registering for the Selective Service

Even if your son has a disability, he must register for the Selective Service. This must be done within thirty days of his eighteenth birthday. The issue of his ability to serve would be addressed if and when the draft is ever activated. (There has not been a draft in over 30 years.) The registration forms can be obtained at any post office or by calling 1-888-655-1825. Your son can mail the completed forms or register online (http://www.sss.gov). After your son has registered, he will receive written confirmation and be assigned a selective service number.

30

Massachusetts Identification Cards

In these times of heightened security, everyone age 18 or older must show photo identification in order to travel by airplane or train. Not just any photo identification card will do—a government issued identification card is needed. The Massachusetts Registry of Motor Vehicles issues a card that satisfies this requirement. You can obtain the card from the Registry of Motor Vehicles. The procedure to obtain the card, including a list of the documents needed to apply, is explained on the Registry's website (http://www.mass.gov.rmv).

31

Chapter 688 Transition Planning for Adult Services

When your son or daughter reaches age 18, the end of special education entitlement may not seem very far away. As every parent knows, age 22 is the line of demarcation where special education services end and adult programs begin. However, some children graduate from special education before their 22nd birthdays—some as early as age 18. If you believe that your son or daughter will need support services when special education ends, you should begin to plan well before he or she is due to graduate. To assist parents and state agencies with planning, Massachusetts has developed a transition process known as Chapter 688. The name is based on the Massachusetts law that oversees and funds transition services.

What does Chapter 688 provide?

Under Chapter 688, a student is assisted in moving from special education services to adult life. Planning must begin when the student is age 14. A lead agency (such as the Department of Mental Health or Department of Developmental Services) is identified that will assist the student as an adult. That agency develops a transition plan that identifies the services the student will need when he or she leaves special education. These services are embodied in a written plan called an Individual Transition Plan (ITP). The ITP describes the student's interests, skills, and needs. It also includes the supports the student will need as an adult. The ITP focuses on three main areas: living situation; day or vocational supports; and ancillary services (such as physical or occupational therapy). The ITP is developed at a meeting that includes the student (if he or she is able to participate), parents, school personnel, and a representative of the lead agency.

Who is eligible for Chapter 688 services?

To be eligible for Chapter 688 services, a person must:

- Be receiving special education services
- Need support services after turning 22 or completing special education
- Be unable to work competitively (that is, without support services) for more than 20 hours per week when leaving school

A person is automatically eligible for Chapter 688 services if he or she receives SSI or SSDI or is registered with the Massachusetts Commission for the Blind. Otherwise, the person's eligibility must be determined. This is done by the 688 Eligibility Unit that is located at the Massachusetts Rehabilitation Commission.

How does the referral process work?

The 688 referral process begins with the student's school system. The special education department selects the adult services agency (such as the Department of Developmental Services or the Massachusetts Commission for the Blind) that might best meet the student's needs as an adult and then makes a referral to that agency. Timing is important for the 688 referral. It should be done before your son or daughter reaches age 18. Thus, if your school system has not made the referral by that time, you should remind the special education director to do so.

Appendices

Appendix A:
Massachusetts Legal Services Offices and Advocacy Organizations that Assist People with Disabilities

These organizations provide free legal services to individuals who have low income and meet other requirements.

Massachusetts Legal Services Offices and Advocacy Organizations that Assist People with Disabilities

Boston College Legal Assistance Bureau
24 Crescent St., Suite 202
Waltham, MA 02453
781-893-4793
781-736-9006 TTY

service areas: Newton, Waltham, Watertown

Children's Law Center
P.O. Box 710
298 Union St.
Lynn, MA 01903
781-581-1977
http://www.clcm.org

service areas: statewide

Community Legal Services and Counseling Center
One West St.
Cambridge, MA 02139
617-661-1010
http://www.clsacc.org

service areas: Arlington, Belmont, Boston, Brookline, Cambridge, Chelsea, Everett, Medford, Somerville, Watertown

Disability Law Center
11 Beacon St., Suite 925
Boston, MA 02108
617-723-8455
800-872-9992

617-227-9464 TTY
800-381-0577 TTY
http://www.dlc-ma.org

service areas: statewide

Disability Law Center
32 Industrial Drive East
Northampton, MA 01060
413-584-6337
800-222-5619
413-582-6919 TTY
http://www.dlc-ma.org

service areas: statewide

Greater Boston Legal Services
197 Friend St.
Boston, MA 02114
617-371-1234
800-323-3205
617-371-1228 TTY
http://www.gbls.org

service areas: Boston, Braintree, Brookline, Canton, Chelsea, Cohasset, Everett, Hingham, Holbrook, Hull, Malden, Medford, Melrose, Milton, Newton, Norwell, Quincy, Randolph, Revere, Scituate, Stoneham, Wakefield, Waltham, Watertown, Weymouth, Winthrop

Cambridge and Somerville Legal Services
60 Gore St., Suite 3
Cambridge, MA 02141
617-603-2700
617-494-1757 TTY
http://www.gbls.org

service areas: Arlington, Belmont, Cambridge, Somerville, Winchester, Woburn

Hale and Dorr Legal Services
122 Boylston St.
Jamaica Plain, MA 02130
617-522-3003
http://www.law.harvard.edu/academics/clinical/lsc

service areas: Jamaica Plain, Roxbury, Dorchester, Mattapan, Roslindale, West Roxbury, Hyde Park

Legal Advocacy and Resource Center
197 Friend St., 9th floor
Boston, MA 02114
617-371-1123
617-603-1700
800-342-5297
http://www.larcma.org

Legal Assistance Corporation of Central Massachusetts

405 Main St., 4th floor
Worcester, MA 01608
508-752-3718
800-649-3718
508-755-3260 TTY
http://www.laccm.org

service areas: Asburnham, Athol, Auburn, Barre, Berlin, Blackstone, Bolton, Boylston, Brookfield, Charlton, Clinton, Douglas, Dudley, East Brookfield, Fitchburg, Gardner, Grafton, Hardwick, Harvard, Holden, Hopedale, Hubbardston, Lancaster, Leicester, Leominster, Lunenburg, Mendon, Milford, Millbury, Millville, New Braintree, North Brookfield, Northborough, Northbridge, Oakham, Oxford, Paxton, Petersham, Phillipston, Princeton, Royalston, Rutland, Shrewsbury, Southborough, Southbridge, Spencer, Sterling, Sturbridge, Sutton, Templeton, Upton, Uxbridge, Warren, West Boylston, West Brookfield, Webster, Westborough, Westminster, Winchendon, Worcester

Legal Services for Cape, Plymouth, and Islands, Inc.
460 West Main St.
Hyannis, MA 02601
508-775-7020
800-742-4107
508-775-7020 TTY
http://www.lscpi.org

service areas: Aquinnah, Barnstable, Bourne, Brewster, Chatham, Chilmark, Dennis, Eastham, Edgartown, Falmouth, Gosnold, Harwich, Hyannis, Mashpee, Nantucket, Oak Bluffs, Orleans, Provincetown, Sandwich, Tisbury, Truro, Wellfleet, West Tisbury, Yarmouth

Legal Services for Cape, Plymouth, and Islands, Inc.
18 Main St. Extension
Plymouth, MA 02360
508-746-2777
800-585-4933
http://www.lscpi.org

service areas: Carver, Duxbury, Halifax, Hanson, Kingston, Lakeville, Marion, Marshfield, Middleborough, Pembroke, Plymouth, Plympton, Rochester, Wareham

Merrimack Valley Legal Services
170 Common St., Suite 303
Lawrence, MA 01840
978-687-1177
800-427-2521
978-689-7275 TTY
http://www.mvlegal.org

service areas: Amesbury, Andover, Beverly, Boxford, Danvers, Essex, Georgetown, Gloucester, Groveland, Hamilton, Haverhill, Ipswich, Lawrence, Lynn, Lynnfield, Manchester, Marblehead, Merrimac, Methuen, Middleton, Nahant, Newbury/Byfield, Newburyport, North Andover, Peabody, Rockport, Rowley, Salem, Salisbury, Saugus, Swampscott, Topsfield, Wenham, West Newbury

Merrimack Valley Legal Services

35 John St., Suite 302
Lowell, MA 01852
978-458-1465
978-458-7701
800-336-2262
978-452-4740 TTY
http://www.mvlegal.org

service areas: Ashby, Ayer, Billerica, Boxborough, Burlington, Chelmsford, Dracut, Dunstable, Groton, Littleton, Lowell, North Reading, Pepperell, Reading, Shirley, Tewksbury, Townsend, Tyngsborough, Westford, Wilmington

Neighborhood Legal Services

170 Common St., Suite 300
Lawrence, MA 01840-1507
978-686-6900
http://www.neighborhoodlaw.org

service areas: Amesbury, Andover, Boxford, Georgetown, Groveland, Haverhill, Lawrence, Merrimac, Methuen, Newbury/Byfield, Newburyport, North Andover, Rowley, Salisbury, West Newbury

Neighborhood Legal Services

37 Friend St.
Lynn, MA 01902
781-599-7730
800-747-5056
781-599-7730 TTY
http://www.neighborhoodlaw.org

service areas: Beverly, Danvers, Essex, Gloucester, Hamilton, Ipswich, Lynn, Lynnfield, Manchester, Marblehead, Middleton, Nahant, Peabody, Rockport, Salem, Saugus, Swampscott, Topsfield, Wenham

Southeastern Massachusetts Legal Assistance Corporation
231 Main St., Suite 201
Brockton, MA 02301
508-586-2110
800-244-8393

service areas: Abington, Attleboro, Avon, Bridgewater, Brockton, East Bridgewater, Easton, Hanover, Mansfield, North Attleboro, Rehoboth, Rockland, Stoughton, West Bridgewater, Whitman

Southeastern Massachusetts Legal Assistance Corporation
22 Bedford St.
Fall River, MA 02720
508-676-6265
800-287-3777

service areas: Berkley, Dighton, Fall River, Freetown, Raynham, Seekonk, Somerset, Swansea, Taunton, Westport

Southeastern Massachusetts Legal Assistance Corporation
21 South Sixth St.
New Bedford, MA 02740
508-979-7150
800-929-9721
508-979-7150 TTY

service areas: Acushnet, Dartmouth, Fairhaven, Gosnold, Marion, Mattapoisett, New Bedford, Rochester

South Middlesex Legal Services
354 Waverly St.
Framingham, MA 01701
508-620-1830
800-696-1501
http://www.smlegal.org

service areas: Acton, Ashland, Bedford, Bellingham, Carlisle, Concord, Dedham, Dover, Foxborough, Framingham, Franklin, Holliston,

Hopkinton, Hudson, Lexington, Lincoln, Marlborough, Maynard, Medfield, Medway, Millis, Natick, Needham, Norfolk, Norwood, Plainville, Sharon, Sherborn, Stow, Sudbury, Walpole, Wayland, Wellesley, Weston, Westwood, Wrentham

Appendix B:
Aging Service Access Points (ASAP) Participating Agencies

You apply for the Adult Family Care Program through the Aging Service Access Point that covers your geographic area. The Adult Family Care Program is covered in Chapter 10, "SSDI, Medicare, MassHealth, and Related Programs."

Aging Service Access Points (ASAP): Participating Agencies

Bay Path Elder Services
33 Boston Post Road West
Marlborough, MA 01752-1853
(508) 573-7200
(800) 287-7284 (toll free)
http://www.baypath.org

Communities served: Ashland, Dover, Framingham, Holliston, Hopkinton, Hudson, Marlborough, Natick, Northborough, Sherborn, Southborough, Sudbury, Wayland, Westborough

Boston ElderINFO
89 South Street
Boston, MA 02111
(617) 292-6211
http://www.elderinfo.org

Communities served: Boston

Boston Senior Home Care
Lincoln Plaza
89 South Street, 5th Floor
Boston, MA 02111
(617) 451-6400
http://www.bshcinfo.org

Communities served: Beacon Hill, Boston, Charlestown, Dorchester, East Boston, North End, South Boston, South Cove, West End

Bristol Elder Services, Inc.
1 Father DeValles Boulevard, B-8, Suite 101
Fall River, MA 02723
(508) 675-2101
(800) 427-2101 (toll free)
http://www.bristolelder.org

Communities served: Attleboro, Berkley, Dighton, Fall River, Freetown, Mansfield, North Attleboro, Norton, Raynham, Rehoboth, Somerset, Swansea, Taunton, Westport

Central Boston Elder Services, Inc.
2315 Washington Street
Boston, MA 02119
(617) 277-7416
http://www.elderinfo.org

Communities served: Allston, Back Bay, Boston, Brighton, Fenway, Jamaica Plain, Roxbury, South End

Central Mass. Agency on Aging, Inc. (AAA)
360 West Boylston Street
West Boylston, MA 01583
(508) 852-5539
(800) 244-3032 (toll free)
http://www.SeniorConnection.org

Communities served: Ashburnham, Ashby, Auburn, Ayer, Barre, Bellingham, Berlin, Blackstone, Bolton, Boylston, Brookfield, Charlton, Douglas, Dudley, East Brookfield, Fitchburg, Franklin, Gardner, Grafton, Groton, Hardwick, Holden, Hopedale, Hubbardston, Lancaster, Leicester, Leominster, Lunenburg, Medway, Mendon, Milford, Millbury, Millville, New Braintree, North Brookfield, Northbridge, Oakham, Oxford, Paxton, Pepperell, Princeton, Rutland, Shirley, Shrewsbury, Southbridge, Spencer, Sterling, Sturbridge, Sutton, Templeton, Townsend, Upton, Uxbridge, Warren, Webster, West Boylston, West Brookfield, Westminster, Winchendon, Worcester

Chelsea/Revere/Winthrop Home Care Center, Inc.
P.O. Box 6427
100 Everett Avenue, Unit 10
Chelsea, MA 02150
(617) 884-2500
http://www.crwelderservices.org

Communities served: Chelsea, Revere, Winthrop

Coastline Elderly Services, Inc.
1646 Purchase Street
New Bedford, MA 02740
(508) 999-6400
http://www.coastlineelderly.org

Communities served: Acushnet, Dartmouth, Fairhaven, Gosnold, Marion, Mattapoisett, New Bedford, Rochester

Commission on Affairs of the Elderly
Boston City Hall
One City Hall Plaza, Room 271
Boston, MA 02201
(617) 635-4366
(617) 635-4646 (Hotline)
(617) 635-4599 (TDD)
elderly@ci.boston.ma.us

Communities served: Boston

Elder Services of Berkshire County, Inc.
66 Wendell Avenue
Pittsfield, MA 01201
(413) 499-0524
(800) 544-5242 (toll free)
http://www.esbci.org

Communities served: Adams. Alford, Becket, Cheshire, Clarksburg, Dalton, Egremont, Florida, Great Barrington, Hancock, Hinsdale,

Lanesborough, Lee, Lenox, Monterey, Mount Washington, New Ashford, New Marlborough, North Adams, Otis, Pittsfield, Richmond, Sandisfield, Savoy, Sheffield, Stockbridge, Tyringham, West Stockbridge, Williamstown, Windsor

Elder Services of Cape Cod and the Islands, Inc.
68 Route 134
South Dennis, MA 02660
(508) 394-4630
http://www.escci.org

Communities served: Aquinnah, Barnstable, Bourne, Brewster, Buzzards Bay, Chatham, Chilmark, Dennis, Eastham, Edgartown, Falmouth, Harwich, Hyannis, Mashpee, Nantucket, Oak Bluffs, Orleans, Provincetown, Sandwich, Tisbury, Truro, Wellfleet, Tisbury, Yarmouth

Elder Services of Merrimack Valley, Inc.
Riverwalk, Building #5
360 Merrimack Street
Lawrence, MA 01843
(978) 683-7747
(800) 892-0890 (toll free)
http://www.esmv.org

Communities served: Amesbury, Andover, Billerica, Boxford, Chelmsford, Dracut, Dunstable, Georgetown, Groveland, Haverhill, Lawrence, Lowell, Merrimack, Methuen, Newbury, Newburyport, North Andover, Rowley, Salisbury, Tewksbury, Tyngsboro, West Newbury, Westford

Elder Services of Worcester Area, Inc.
411 Chandler Street
Worcester, MA 01602
(508) 756-1545
http://www.eswa.org

Communities served: Auburn, Barre, Boylston, Grafton, Hardwick,

Holden, Leicester, Millbury, New Braintree, Oakham, Paxton, Rutland, Shrewsbury, West Boylston, Worcester

Ethos
555 Amory Street
Jamaica Plain, MA 02130
(617) 522-6700
(617) 524-2687 (TDD)
http://www.ethocare.org

Communities served: Boston, Hyde Park, Jamaica Plain, Mattapan, Roslindale, West Roxbury

Franklin County Home Care Corporation
330 Montague City Road
Turners Falls, MA 01373
(413) 773-5555
http://www.fchcc.org

Communities served: Ashfield, Athol, Bernardston, Buckland, Charlemont, Colrain, Conway, Deerfield, Erving, Gill, Greenfield, Hawley, Heath, Leverett, Leyden, Monroe, Montague, New Salem, Northfield, Orange, Petersham, Phillipston, Rowe, Royalston, Shelburne, Shutesbury, Sunderland, Warwick, Wendell, Whately

Greater Lynn Senior Services, Inc.
8 Silsbee Street
Lynn, MA 01901
(781) 599-0110
(781) 477-9632 (TDD)
http://www.glss.net

Communities served: Lynn, Lynnfield, Nahant, Saugus, Swampscott

Greater Springfield Senior Services, Inc.
66 Industry Avenue
Springfield, MA 01104
(413) 781-8800

(800) 649-3641 (toll free)
(413) 272-0399 (TTY)
http://www.gsssi.org

Communities served: Agawam, Brimfield, East Longmeadow, Hampden, Holland, Longmeadow, Monson, Palmer, Springfield, Wales, West Springfield, Wilbraham

HESSCO Elder Services
One Merchant Street
Sharon, MA 02067
(781) 784-4944
(800) 462-5221 (toll free)
http://www.hessco.org

Communities served: Canton, Dedham, Foxborough, Medfield, Millis, Norfolk, Norwood, Plainville, Sharon, Walpole, Westwood, Wrentham

Highland Valley Elder Services, Inc.
320 Riverside Drive, Suite B
Florence, MA 01062
(413) 586-2000
(800) 322-0551 (toll free)
http://www.highlandvalley.org

Communities served: Amherst, Blandford, Chester, Chesterfield, Cummington, Easthampton, Goshen, Granville, Hadley, Hatfield, Huntington, Middlefield, Montgomery, Northampton, Pelham, Plainfield, Russell, Southampton, Southwick, Tolland, Westfield, Westhampton, Williamsburg, Worthington

Minuteman Senior Services
24 Third Avenue
Burlington, MA 01803
(781) 272-7177
http://www.minutemansenior.org

Communities served: Acton, Arlington, Bedford, Boxborough, Burlington, Carlisle, Concord, Harvard, Lexington, Lincoln, Littleton, Maynard, Stow, Wilmington, Winchester, Woburn

Montachusett Home Care Corporation
Crossroads Office Park
Leominster, MA 01453
(978) 537-7411
(800) 734-7312 (toll free)
http://www.montachusetthomecare.com

Communities served: Ashburnham, Ashby, Ayer, Berlin, Bolton, Clinton, Fitchburg, Gardner, Groton, Hubbardston, Lancaster, Leominster, Pepperell, Princeton, Shirley, Sterling, Templeton, Townsend, Westminster, Winchendon

Mystic Valley Elder Services, Inc.
300 Commercial Street, Suite #19
Malden, MA 02148
(781) 324-7705
http://www.mves.org

Communities served: Everett, Malden, Medford, Melrose, North Reading, Reading, Stoneham, Wakefield

North Shore Elder Services, Inc.
152 Sylvan Street
Danvers, MA 01923
(978) 750-4540
(978) 624-2244 (TDD/TTY)
http://www.nselder.org

Communities served: Danvers, Marblehead, Middleton, Peabody, Salem

Old Colony Elder Services, Inc.
144 Main Street
Brockton, MA 02301

(508) 584-1561
(800) 242-0246 (toll free)
http://www.oc-elder.org

Communities served: Abington, Avon, Bridgewater, Brockton, Carver, Duxbury, East Bridgewater, Easton, Halifax, Hanover, Hanson, Kingston, Lakeville, Marshfield, Middleborough, Pembroke, Plymouth, Plympton, Rockland, Stoughton, Wareham, West Bridgewater, Whitman

Old Colony Planning Council
70 School Street
Brockton, MA 02301
(508) 583-1833
http://www.ocpcrpa.org

Communities served: Abington, Avon, Bridgewater, Brockton, Carver, Duxbury, Halifax, Hanover, Hanson, Kingston, Lakeville, Marshfield, Middleborough, Pembroke, Plymouth, Plympton, Rockland, Stoughton, Wareham, West Bridgewater, Whitman

SeniorCare, Inc.
5 Blackburn Center
Gloucester, MA 01930
(978) 281-1750
http://www.seniorcareinc.org

Communities served: Beverly, Essex, Gloucester, Hamilton, Ipswich, Manchester-by-the-Sea, Rockport, Topsfield, Wenham

Somerville/Cambridge Elder Services, Inc.
61 Medford Street
Somerville, MA 02143
(617) 628-2601
(617) 628-2602
(617) 628-1705 (TDD)
http://www.eldercare.org

Communities served: Cambridge, Somerville

South Shore Elder Services, Inc.
159 Bay State Drive
Braintree, MA 02184
(781) 749-6832
(781) 383-9790
(781) 848-3910
http://www.sselder.org

Communities served: Braintree, Cohasset, Hingham, Holbrook, Hull, Milton, Norwell, Quincy, Randolph, Scituate, Weymouth

Springwell, Inc.
125 Walnut Street
Watertown, MA 02472
(617) 926-4100
http://www.springwell.com

Communities served: Belmont, Brookline, Needham, Newton, Waltham, Watertown, Wellesley, Weston

Tri-Valley, Inc.
10 Mill Street
Dudley, MA 01571
(508) 949-6640
(800) 286-6640 (toll free)
http://www.tves.org/home.html

Communities served: Bellingham, Blackstone, Brookfield, Charlton, Douglas, Dudley, East Brookfield, Franklin, Hopedale, Medway, Mendon, Milford, Millville, North Brookfield, Northbridge, Oxford, Southbridge, Spencer, Sturbridge, Sutton, Upton, Uxbridge, Warren, Webster, West Brookfield

WestMass Elder Care, Inc.
4 Valley Mill Road
Holyoke, MA 01040
(413) 538-9020
(800) 462-2301 (toll free)

(800) 875-0287 (V/TDD)
http://www.wmeldercare.org

Communities served: Belchertown, Chicopee, Granby, Holyoke, Ludlow, South Hadley, Ware

Appendix C: Antipsychotic and Other Medications Used to Treat People with Mental Illness

If a person under guardianship takes any antipsychotic medication, the guardian must obtain special authority from the probate court to administer such medication. This is called a *Rogers* guardianship. (See Chapter 15, "Special Situations.") A guardian does NOT need special authority to administer an anti-depressant or mood stabilizing drug.

Antipsychotic and Other Medications Used to Treat People With Mental Illness

Antipsychotics

Brand name	Generic name	Usual daily dose (mg)
Abilify	Aripiprazole	10-15
Clozaril	Clozapine	300-900
Geodon	Ziprasidone	40-160
Haldol	Haloperidol	1-15
Loxitane	Loxapine	60-100
Mellaril	Thioridazine	150-800
Moban	Molindone	50-225
Navane	Thiothixene	6-60
Orap	Pimozide	2-10
Prolixin	Fluphenazine	2-20
Risperdal	Risperidone	2-8
Serentil	Mesoridazine	100-400
Seroquel	Quetiapine fumarate	300-750
Stelazine	Trifluoperazine	15-40
Thorazine	Chlorpromazine	30-75
Trilafon	Perphenazine	12-64
Zyprexa	Olanzapine	10-20

Antidepressants

Brand name	Generic name	Usual daily dose (mg)
Celexa	Citalopram	20-40
Desyrel	Trazodone	150-400
Effexor	Venlaxafine	75-375
Elavil	Amitriptyline	50-200
Luvox	Fluvoxamine	100-300
Nardil	Phenelzine	45-90
Norpramin	Desipramine	100-300
Parnate	Tranylcypromine	30-60
Paxil	Paroxetine	20-60
Proxac	Fluoxetine	20-60
Remeron	Mirtazapine	15-45
Serzone	Nefazodone	200-600
Sinequan	Doxepin	75-150
Tofranil	Imipramine	75-200
Vivactil	Protriptyline	15-60
Wellbutrin	Bupropion	200-450
Zoloft	Sertraline	50-200

Mood Stabilizers

Brand name	Generic name	Usual daily dose (mg)
Depakote	Divalproex sodium	500-1,000
Eskalith; Lithonate	Lithium carbonate	900-1,800
Klonopin	Clonazepam	1.5-4
Lamictal	Lamotrizine	100-500
Neurontin	Gabapentin	300-1,800
Tegretol	Carbatrol	200-1,200

Appendix D:
Medical Release and
Authorization Form

By signing a Medical Release and Authorization form, a person can permit third parties to review private medical information. In some cases, this can avoid guardianship. The form can be modified to fit the person's circumstances. See Chapter 12, "Alternatives to Guardianship."

<u>MEDICAL RELEASE AND AUTHORIZATION</u>

TO:

FROM:

    I, _____, of_____ _____ hereby authorize you to release any and all of my medical records to my agent(s) _____, of _____ _____ _____. My agent(s) may obtain copies of my medical records on request. I also authorize you to discuss my medical care with my agent(s).

    I intend that this release authority shall apply to any information governed by the Health Insurance Portability and Accountability Act of 1996 (HIPPA).

    This Release shall remain in effect until it is revoked by me.

Date:_____   _____

                                   (Signature)

Appendix E:
Authorization for Guardian
to Delegate to Caregiver

This Authorization form can be used by guardians who are participating in the Adult Family Care Program. It can allow a spouse or other close relative to act on behalf of a person under guardianship in the guardian's absence. The Adult Family Care Program is covered in Chapter 10, "SSDI, Medicare, MassHealth, and Related Programs."

AUTHORIZATION

I, _____ of _____, as the legal guardian of _____,

Hereby authorize _____ of _____, to do the following on behalf of _____ :

1. consent to routine medical care
2. consent to emergency care
3. review all school, medical, dental, psychological, psychiatric, and other records, reports or written communications concerning _____
4. consult with individuals providing medical, psychological, psychiatric medical, dental, therapeutic, educational or other services to _____
5. receive information from, and communicate information to, medical insurance providers that provide services to _____, either directly or as a covered individual under any medical insurance policy of mine
6. consent to recreational activities
7. exercise sole authority and responsibility for decisions concerning _____'s daily living needs and social activities
8. apply for and manage public benefits on behalf of _____
9. do and authorize all things that I could do and authorize as _____'s legal guardian.

Witness my hand and seal this _____ day of _____, 200_.

_____
(print name)
LEGAL GUARDIAN OF

COMMONWEALTH OF MASSACHUSETTS

County of

On this _____ day of _____, 200_, before me, the undersigned notary, personally appeared _____, proved to me through satisfactory evidence of identification, which were _____, to be the person whose name is signed on the preceding or attached document, and acknowledged to me that s/he signed it voluntarily for its stated purpose.

_____

My Commission Expires:

Appendix F:
Pooled Trusts in Massachusetts

Third party trusts

CJP Disabilities Trust
Jewish Family & Children's Service
1430 Main St.
Waltham, MA 02451
781-647-5327
http://www.jfcsboston.org

PLAN of Massachusetts Third Party Special Needs Pooled Trust
PLAN of Massachusetts, Inc.
1301 Centre St.
Newton, MA 02451
617-244-5552
http://www.planofma.org

First party trusts

Berkshire County Arc Master Special Needs Pooled Trust
Berkshire County Arc, Inc.
395 South St.
Pittsfield, MA 01201
413-499-4241
http://www.bcarc.org

PLAN of Massachusetts Special Needs Pooled Trust
(MARC Trust)
PLAN of Massachusetts, Inc.
1301 Centre St.
Newton, MA 02451
617-244-5552
http://www.planofma.org

Family Trust of Massachusetts
Charles N. Gallo, Administrator
84 State St. – Suite 1100
Boston, MA 02109
peter@macylaw.com

Resources

Useful Books, Government Agencies, and Other Resources

Books

An Advocate's Guide to Surviving the SSI System. Linda L. Landry, et al, Disability Law Center, Massachusetts Law Reform Institute, and Massachusetts Continuing Legal Institute, Inc. (2002). Also known as "the Yellow Book." This book has not been updated since 2002. However, it is still a valuable resource guide to SSI appeals and the SSI financial and disability rules. $15. Order from Massachusetts Continuing Legal Education (MCLE), 10 Winter Place, Boston, MA. 02108. 1-800-966-6253. http://www.mcle.org.

Handbook on Guardianship of Nursing Home Residents in Massachusetts: Demystifying Guardianship and Long-Term Care Medicaid. John J. Ford, iUniverse (2005). This useful book contains much practical information on the Massachusetts court process, the appointment of guardians, and *Rogers* monitors. It also explains the guardian's responsibilities. $20.95. Order from Amazon.com or any online book publisher.

Living Trust, Living Hell. John P. Huggard, Parker-Thompson Publishing (2004). This exposé-type book reveals why most people probably do not need a living trust. $25. Order from amazon.com or any online book publisher.

Managing a Special Needs Trust: A Guide for Trustees. Barbara D. Jackins, et al (2010). This is a practical reference guide for trustees of special needs trusts. Order from DisABILITIESBOOKS.com or Amazon.com. $24.95

Publications

The Massachusetts Department of Mental Health's Human Rights Handbook. This handbook is a companion to the DMH Humans Right Policy. It explains the regulations and policies for DMH facilities. A comprehensive appendix contains DMH human rights policy, charts, forms, documents, and advocacy resources. Order online at http://www.mass.gov/dmh or from the Massachusetts Department of Mental Health, 25 Staniford St., Boston, MA 02114.

Mental Health Law Guide. Mental Health Legal Advisors Committee. A collection of MHLAC's most requested pamphlets. The topics include involuntary hospitalization, the right to obtain mental health records, a patient's basic rights at mental health facilities, etc. $35. Order from MHLAC, 399 Washington St., 4th floor, Boston, MA 02108. 617-338-2345.

Passport to Independence: A Manual for Families. Specialized Housing, Inc., Cynthia Haddad, and John Nadworny. A manual of information on planning for independence, including financial planning, supported housing, and social and vocational issues. Written by and for families. $15 plus $5 shipping and handling. Order from Specialized Housing, Inc., 45 Bartlett Crescent, Brookline, MA 02446. 617-277-1805

Red Book on Employment. Publication 64-030 of the Social Security Administration: Guide to Social Security work-related rules and regulations. Obtain from the SSA website (http://www.ssa.gov) or by telephone 800-772-1213.

Section 8 Made Simple. Technical Assistance Collaborative, Inc. (2003). Excellent reader-friendly guide to the Section 8 program. Order from TAC by telephone 617-266-5657 or from its website (http://www.tacinc.org).

Special Needs Planning Guide. A five-chapter pamphlet on special needs planning. Chapters by Patricia Freedman, Cynthia Haddad, Harry S. Margolis, and Patricia Freedman. $15. Order from Jewish Family &

Children's Services, ATTN: Ilana Gordon-Brown, 1340 Centre St., Newton, MA 02459.

Special Needs Planning Guide: How to Prepare for Every Stage of your Child's Life. By John W. Nadworny and Cynthia R. Haddad. Brookes Publishing Company, 2007. This practical book covers the financial, legal, and emotional aspects of planning for a child with special needs. Order from the authors at specialneedsplanning.com or from any online bookseller.

Supplemental Security Income. Publication 05-11000 of the Social Security Administration. General guide to the SSI program. Order from the SSA website (http://www.ssa.gov) or by telephone. 800-772-1213.

Ticket to Work and Self-sufficiency Program. Publication 05-10068 of the Social Security Administration. Obtain from the SSA website (http://www.ssa.gov) or by calling the Social Security Administration. 800-772-1213.

Federal Government Resources

Social Security Administration. http://www.ssa.gov. Telephone 800-772-1213. The toll-free number is staffed 24 hours a day, including weekends and holidays.

Center for Medicare and Medicaid Services. http://www.medicare. gov. Telephone 800-MEDICARE. The toll-free number is staffed 24 hours a day, including weekends and holidays.

Center for Medicare Advocacy, Inc. http://www.medicareadvocacy. org. An advocacy organization for Medicare recipients. This organization provides helpful information about the new Medicare drug benefit.

Massachusetts Government Resources

Disabled Persons Protection Commission. The Massachusetts Commission empowered to protect adults with disabilities from abuse.

50 Ross Way, Quincy, MA 02169. 617-727-6465. Hotline: 800-426-9009.

Massachusetts Commission for the Blind. The state agency that provides services to the blind. Executive office: 48 Boylston St., Boston, MA 02116. 617-727-5550; 800-392-6450; 800-392-6556 (TDD). http://www.mass.gov/dma.

Massachusetts Commission for the Deaf and Hard of Hearing. The state agency that provides services to people who are deaf and heard of hearing. Executive office: 150 Mount Vernon St., fifth floor, Dorchester, MA 02125. http://www.mass.gov/mcdhh.

Massachusetts Department of Developmental Services. The state agency that oversees services to individuals with intellectual disabilities. 500 Harrison Ave., Boston, MA 02108. 617-210-5000. http://www.mass/gov.dds.

Massachusetts Department of Mental Health. The state agency that oversees services to individuals with mental illness. Central office: 25 Staniford St., Boston, MA 02114. 617-626-8000; 617-727-9842 (TTY). http://www.mass.gov/dmh.

Massachusetts Department of Public Health, Division of Special Health Needs. The state office that coordinates care for children with special health needs such as a chronic illness, disabling condition, or a frequent need for medical technology. Bureau of Family and Community Health, 250 Washington St., Boston, MA 02108. 617-624-5966; 617-624-5992 (TTY). http://www.mass.gov/dph/fch.

Massachusetts Division of Medical Assistance. The state office that oversees the MassHealth program. One Ashburton Place, 11th floor, Boston, MA 02108. Customer Service 800-841-2900. http://www.mass.gov/dma.

Massachusetts Rehabilitation Commission. Government office that provides employment and independent living services to residents with disabilities. Main office: Fort Point Place, 27 Wormwood St., Boston,

MA 02210. 800-245-6543 or 617-204-3600. http://www.mass.gov/mrc.

Legal Resources

Probate court forms: Guardianship and conservatorship forms are available on the Massachusetts probate and family court website, http://www.mass.gov/courts/courtsandjudges/courts/probateandfamilycourt.html.

National Academy of Elder Law Attorneys. A national organizations of attorneys who specialize in elder and disability law. The staff can help you locate an attorney in your area. 1604 Country Club Road, Tucson, AZ 85716. 520-881-4005. http://www.naela.org.

The trial court libraries contain all current Massachusetts laws and regulations. http://www.lawlib.state.ma.us.

A compendium of all disability laws in the Commonwealth of Massachusetts is located at. http://www.state.ma.us/mod/msdislaw.html.

Other Resources

National Information Center for Children and Youth with Disabilities (NICHCY). A national clearinghouse for information related to disabilities in children and youth. P.O. Box 1492, Washington, DC 20013. 800-695-0285. nichy@aed.org.

New England INDEX. Provides information for people in New England with disabilities. An extensive database of providers such as programs, agencies, physicians, dentists, and consultants. Located at the Eunice Kennedy Shriver Center, 200 Trapelo Road, Waltham, MA 02452. 781-642-0248, 800-642-0248. http://www.disabilityinfo.org.

Glossary

Account In the trust context, a summary of the financial activity of a trust for a particular period of time, usually a year. In the probate context, a summary of the income and expenses related to assets managed by a guardian, trustee, administrator, executor, or conservator.

Administrator A person appointed by the probate court to oversee and distribute the property of someone who dies without a valid will.

Agent A person who is given authority by another person (the principal) to act on his or her behalf.

Antipsychotic medication Medications that are used to treat the symptoms of mental illness. A guardian should not permit the person under his or her care to be treated with antipsychotic medications without first obtaining a court order.

Beneficiary A person or organization that receives benefits under a will or trust. The term also refers to a person or organization that will receive the proceeds of a life insurance policy, retirement account, or annuity when the owner dies.

Bond In the guardianship context, a pledge that a person will faithfully perform his or her guardianship duties. A guardian's bond must be approved by the probate court.

Bypass trust A trust that married couples can use to reduce estate taxes. Property that one spouse leaves for the surviving spouse in a bypass trust is not included in the surviving spouse's estate for estate tax purposes. Also called a family trust or credit shelter trust.

Citation A legal notice issued by the court in a guardianship case. The citation must be given to the people and agencies listed on the form.

Clinical team report A document that must be filed with the probate court in order for a guardian to be appointed for person with mental retardation. The clinical team report must be signed by a physician, a licensed psychologist, and a licensed social worker.

Contingent beneficiary An alternate person or organization named to receive property if the primary beneficiary is no longer living when benefits become payable.

Co-trustees Two or more individuals or organizations that serve as trustees of a trust at the same time.

Corporate trustee A bank, trust company, or other financial organization that specializes in managing trusts.

Credit shelter trust See *by-pass trust*.

Custodian A person named to manage property for a minor under the Uniform Transfers to Minors Act (UTMA).

Decree A judgment issued by a court. In a guardianship case, the judge signs a guardianship decree appointing one or more persons to be legal guardians.

Disabled adult child (DAC) The disabled son or daughter of a person who receives Social Security benefits. The disabled son or daughter must have been continuously disabled since before the age of twenty-two.

Durable power of attorney A power of attorney that remains in effect even if the person who makes the document later becomes disabled (see power of attorney).

Estate A person's assets or property.

Estate planning The process of managing one's personal property during life time and arranging for its orderly transfer on death.

Estate tax The tax imposed by the federal and state governments on property that a person owns at the time of his or her death.

Executor The person appointed by the probate court to administer the will of a deceased person.

Family trust See by-pass trust.

Fiduciary A person or organization that holds a position of trust and responsibility for another person or organization. Some examples of fiduciaries are guardians, trustees, agents, executors, and administrators.

Funding a trust The process of registering property in the name of the trustee.

Gift tax A federal tax imposed on money or property that a person gives away while he or she is living. A person can give $13,000 per year to an unlimited number of people without incurring a gift tax.

Guardian A person who has been authorized by a court to make decisions on behalf of another person (the Incapacitated Person).

Guardianship, general In Massachusetts, a guardianship in which the guardian makes all major decisions for the person under his or her supervision, including support, care, education, health, and welfare.

Guardian, temporary A guardian who has been appointed to act for only 90 days. This can be a guardian of the person or the estate.

Guardianship, limited In Massachusetts, a guardianship in which the guardian makes some but not all personal decisions for the Incapacitated Person. For example, the guardian might only decide the Incapacitated Person's medical care, but the Incapacitated Person would make all other personal decisions.

Health care proxy A document by which a person (the principal) gives another person (the agent) the right to make health care decisions for the principal.

Incapacitated Person A person whom the court has placed under guardianship.

Irrevocable life insurance trust (ILIT) A trust that allows a person to pass the proceeds of a life insurance policy to the beneficiaries estate tax free.

Irrevocable trust A trust that the creator cannot cancel or change.

Joint ownership with rights of survivorship A way that two or more people can own the same asset. When one owner dies, the survivor or survivors automatically own the deceased person's share.

Less restrictive alternative A way that a person with a disability can be assisted without a guardian being appointed. Some examples of less restrictive alternatives are joint ownership of assets, powers of attorney, trusts, and representative payment for government benefits.

Letter of appointment A form the probate court issues stating that a person has been appointed to be the guardian or conservator for another person.

Living Trust A trust that a person creates while he or she is alive.

Living will A written statement about the kind of care that a person would want or not want, such as artificial life supports, if he or she were critically ill.

Marital trust A trust that is established for a spouse in order to obtain certain estate tax benefits.

Medicaid A medical insurance program for poor people that is administered by the states and jointly paid for by the state and federal governments. In Massachusetts, Medicaid is called "MassHealth."

Medical Certificate A document that must be filed with the probate court in order to have a guardian appointed for a person who has mental illness. A Medical Certificate must be signed by a physician and is valid for 30 days.

Medicare A medical insurance program primarily for people who qualify for Social Security benefits. Medicare is funded and administered by the federal government.

Minor In Massachusetts, a person who is under age 18.

Power of Attorney A document by which a person (the principal) gives another person or persons (the agent) authority to act on his or her behalf. Also see Durable Power of Attorney.

Principal A person who gives another person authority to act on his or her behalf.

Probate Court In Massachusetts, a court that oversees guardianship and estate matters.

Protected Person A person with a disability whom the Court has placed under conservatorship.

Revocable trust A trust that the creator can cancel or change.

***Rogers* guardianship** In Massachusetts, a probate court proceeding in which the guardian asks the court to permit a person under guardianship to be treated with antipsychotic medication.

***Rogers* monitor** The person whom the court appoints to oversee the court-ordered antipsychotic medication treatment plan.

Self-funded trust A trust that contains funds that originally belonged to the beneficiary. (Also called a self-settled trust.)

Special needs trust A trust that provides benefits for a person with a disability. The trust funds can be used to pay for goods and services that government programs do not provide.

Successor trustee A person or organization that takes over as the trustee when the former trustee resigns.

Supplemental needs trust See special needs trust.

Surety In the guardianship context, a person or insurance company that acts as a guarantor for a guardian. The surety pledges his or her own property to insure that the guardian will faithfully perform his or her duties.

Tenancy by the entirety A special kind of joint ownership between spouses in which one spouse cannot change the ownership without the other's consent. In Massachusetts, this kind of ownership gives special protection from creditors.

Third party trust A trust that contains funds that originally belonged to someone other than the beneficiary. For example, a parent might establish a third party trust to benefit a son or daughter with a disability.

Treatment Plan In the context of a guardianship, a physician's proposal for the administration of antipsychotic medication. A treatment plan should include the proposed medication; dosage; method of administration (oral, injection, etc.); side effects; risks, benefits; prognosis with treatment; prognosis without treatment; and alternative medications and dosages.

Trustee A person or organization that manages a trust.

Uniform Transfers to Minors Act (UTMA) A law that allows a person to make a gift to a minor by giving the property to a custodian to hold until the minor reaches the age specified in the statute (21 in Massachusetts).

Will A written document by which a person gives instructions for the distribution of property on his or her death.

Index

A

Administrative Law Judge,
   see SSI appeals
Adult Family Care Program,
   78-79, 100
Advocacy organizations, 38, App. A
Aging Service Access Points, 79, App. B
Alimony, 20
Annual report for guardianship
   cases, 118
Antipsychotic medication, 98,
   111-112, 135, App. C
Attorneys,
   court-appointed in guardianship
      cases, 106-107, 108
   guardianship cases, 103-104, 114
   legal services, 38, App. A
   SSI cases, 38
Authorization for Guardian
   to Delegate to Caregiver
   form, 101-102, App. E

B

Bank accounts
   joint, 126, 215
   pay on death, 217
   Representative Payee, 31, 35
Blindness and SSI, 11-12
Bond, *see surety bond*
Burial instructions, 163

C

Care Plan Report for
   guardianship cases, 117
Child support, 18-21
Children
   SSI benefits, 22
   in residential schools, 22
Clinical team report, 104, 105,
   109, 115, 129, 135
Clothing and SSI, 57
Conservatorship, 125, 129-132, 160
   alternatives to, 125-128

court process, 129-131
   for minor children, 160
   reporting requirements, 130-131

D

Directions book, 176
Disabled adult children, 68
Disabled Persons Protection
   Commission, 119-120
Divorced parent, 19, 142, 151-152, 192
Dual recipients of SSI and SSDI, 69-70
Durable power of attorney, 94-95,
   127, 156, 164, 182-184, 194
   springing durable power
      of attorney, 183

E

ECT treatments, 115
Employer Identification Number
   (EIN), 173, 218
Estate tax, 144, 155, 164, 194,
   195, 196, 216, 217
Executor, 156, 162, 164

F

Family limited partnership, 198-199
Financial planner, 154, 185, 209-212
529 college savings plan, 13, 217
Food and SSI, 17, 50, 53, 55, 56, 57, 59
Food stamps, 59

G

Gift tax, 199, 216, 219
Grandparents' gifts, 172, 215-216
Guardianship
   age to apply for, 106
   alternatives to, 91-102
   co-guardians, 134
   emergency, 115
   fees, 123-124
   forms, where to obtain, 104
   kinds of guardianship

general, 87, 99-100, 135
limited, 87, 98-99
Rogers, 98, 103-104,
112-115, 124
Guardian's liability for
person's actions, 123

H

Health Care Proxy, 90, 92-
93, 156, 164, 184
HIPPA, 92-93
Homestead Declaration, 194, 212-213
Housing and SSI, 55, 57-59
Human rights and dignity, 118-120

I

Identification cards, 225
Impairment Related Work
Expenses (IRWE)
see Work
Income
earned income and
SSDI, 70, 71-72
earned income and SSI, 15-16, 70
in-kind income and SSI, 17-18
unearned income and SSDI, 70-71
unearned income and
SSI, 16-17, 70
Income tax
alimony and, 20
Caregiver Homes Program and, 79
retirement accounts and, 151
special needs trust and, 173, 219
personal savings and, 216
Independent medical examination, 32
Informed consent, 120-122

J

Joint ownership of assets, 148,
155, 164, 197, 215

L

Legal aid offices, 38, App. A
Letter of Intent, 164, 177-179
Life insurance, 201-207
cash value and SSI, 13, 30
estate taxes and, 196
joint insurance, 204-205
naming proper beneficiaries,
147, 148, 149-150,
151, 155, 156, 210
second to die policy, 198, 204
term insurance, 202-203
permanent insurance, 203-204
Living trust, *see trusts*
Living Trust, Living Hell, 195
Living will, 156, 164, 184

M

MassHealth, 75-78, 99
CommonHealth, 76-78
SSI and, 8
Standard, 75-76
qualifying without SSI, 9, 76
Medicaid, *see MassHealth*
Medical certificate, 104, 105,
106, 109, 115, 129, 135
Medical release, see *Release for
medical information*
Medicare, 72-75, 76, 99
SSDI and, 71, 186

N

Nursing home costs, 24, 73, 185, 187
special needs payback trust
and, 187-189

P

Pay on death account, 217
Personal Care Attendant
Program, 79-81, 100
Physicians Desk Reference, 112

Plan to Achieve Self Support
    (PASS), *see Work*
Pooled trust, *see trusts*
Probate, 143, 155, 164
    living trust and, 143

Q

QDOT trust, 195

R

Record keeping
    for SSI program, 36, 45
    for guardians, 122-123
    for conservators, 131
    for trustees, 166
Release for medical information,
    91-92, App. D
Representative payee, 31, 33-
    36, 90, 118, 126
    bank account, 31, 35
    liability for overpayment, 48
    report to Social Security, 36
Residential schools, 22
Retirement accounts,
    estate taxes and, 196
    income taxes, 151
    naming proper beneficiaries,
        147, 148, 149-150,
        151, 155, 156, 210
    probate and, 164
Rogers guardianship, see guardianship
Rogers monitor, 110, 113, 114-115, 123

S

Selective Service registration, 223
Side letter
    to a special needs trust,
        164, 176-177
    to a will, 162
Single parents, 153-154
Special needs trust
    as an alternative to
        conservatorship, 127-128

as part of an estate plan, 141,
    142, 146, 152, 156, 165-174
child support and, 18-21
court approval for, 126, 189
durable power of attorney and, 183
irrevocable, 173, 215
"payback" trust, 188, 215
saving money in, 216-217
self-funded, 168
SSDI and, 71
SSI and, 13, 25-28
third party, 168
trustee selection, 156, 166-172
Surety bond, 104
SSDI (Social Security Disability
    Insurance), 67-72
    assets and, 71
    benefit amounts, 69
    compared to SSI (chart), 70
    for previously health
        adults, 185-186
    unearned income, and 71
    Medicare and, 71
    work and, 71-72
SSI (Supplemental Security Income)
    appeals, 37-44
        Administrative Law Judge, 41
        Appeals Council, 43
        Federal Court, 44
        Formal conference, 40
        Informal conference, 40
        Reconsideration, 38
    applying for benefits, 29-32
        by telephone, 30
        information needed, 30-31
        when to apply, 29
        where to apply, 30
    benefit amounts, 7-8
    blind recipients, 11-12
    child support payments and, 18-21
    children in residential schools, 22
    children's benefits, 22
    compared to SSDI (chart), 70
    earned income, 15-16, 62, 70

for previously health
  adults, 185-186
income limits, 15-18
in-kind income, 17
overpayment of benefits, 45-48
reducing assets to qualify, 23-28
repayment of benefits, 45-48
resource limits, 12-13
retroactive payments, 13
state supplement, 8
transfers of assets, 23-24
unearned income, 16-17
Sterilization, 115
Students
  work and, 15, 62
  transition to adult
    services, 227-228
Surety bond, 104-105

T

Tenancy by the entirety, 213-214
Transition planning to adult
  services, 227-228
Trustee
  fees, 169-170
  professional, 169-170
  responsibilities, 166
  successor, 166, 170
Trusts, kinds of,
  bypass, 195-197
  credit shelter, 196-197
  irrevocable, 215, 218-219
  irrevocable life insurance trust
    (ILIT), 197-198, 207
  living, 143, 193-195
  revocable, 160, 191-192, 217-218
  payback, *see special needs trust*
  pooled, 146, 173-174, App. F
  special needs, *see special needs trust*
  testamentary, 160, 191

U

UGMA account, 13, 14
UTMA account, 13-15, 215
  reducing accounts to qualify
    for SSI, 27-28

V

Vacations, 25, 35, 51, 59, 128, 176
Voting and guardianship, 133

W

Wills, 159-164
  advantages,159
  executor, 156, 162-163
  person under guardianship
    and, 133
  limitations, 164
Withdrawal of life support
  by guardian, 115
Work, 61-66
  Impairment Related Work
    Expense (IRWE), 63-64
  Plan to Achieve Self-Support
    (PASS), 13, 64-66
  SSDI and, 71-72
  SSI and, 12, 15-16, 61-63
  student earnings, 15, 62